The Yorkshire Dales

TO

Alyson, Simon, Helen, Robert and Kate
who all suffered from my impromptu lectures
over several otherwise happy Easter holidays
in the Dales.

The Yorkshire Dales

by
J. C. Barringer

Dalesman Books
1982

The Dalesman Publishing Company Ltd.,
Clapham, via Lancaster, LA2 8EB.
First published 1982
© J. C. Barringer, 1982.

ISBN: 0 85206 668 6

Christopher Barringer was educated at Ilkley Grammar School and
St. John's College, Cambridge, where he read geography and took a
post graduate Certificate in Education. He was Senior Geography
Master at Lancaster Royal Grammar School from 1954 to 1965. Since
then he has been Resident Tutor in Norfolk to the University of
Cambridge Board of Extra-Mural Studies, where his teaching and
research interests have focussed increasingly on Local Studies and
Local History in his work with adult students studying the histories of
the villages and market towns of East Anglia.

Printed by Fretwell & Brian Ltd., Healey Works, Goulbourne Street,
Keighley, West Yorkshire BD21 1PZ.

Contents

Cover photograph of Swaledale near Thwaite by Tom Parker.

Sources

THE bibliography for a study such as this is a difficult problem and each chapter has been provided with a main source list. Two major source collections that have provided much material for this book are the works of the Rev. T. D. Whitaker on Craven, Richmond, Loidis and Elmet and Whalley, and secondly the very detailed publications edited by Bernard Jennings on Nidderdale, Harrogate and Knaresborough and that with Roger Fieldhouse on Richmond and Swaledale. These three volumes are a great credit to the work of many adult students who have had the good fortune to be guided by Jennings and Fieldhouse.

The Victoria County History volumes on Yorkshire and on the North Riding contain much basic material and so does the splendid *Directory of Yorkshire* produced by Baines in 1822 and reprinted in 1969. Yorkshire is fortunate in the quality of the *Yorkshire Archaeological Journal* and the very valuable volumes of the Record Series produced by the Archaeological Society and also in the transactions of the Thoresby Society.

Abbreviations

I.B.G. Transactions of the Institute of British Geographers
V.C.H. Victoria County History
Y.A.J. Yorkshire Archaeological Journal
Y.A.S. Yorkshire Archaeological Society
Y.E.C. Yorkshire Early Charters
Y.R.S. Yorkshire Record Series

All photographs unless separately acknowledged were taken by the author.

Photographs from the Cambridge University Collection are by J. K. St. Joseph – Crown copyright reserved.

Introduction

THE Yorkshire Dales, in particular Wharfedale, was the area in which I grew up and spent my school years. It is the area to which fortunately I am still able to return fairly frequently. It was therefore both a challenge and a delight to be asked more years ago than I like to think to try to produce a book in the Dalesman series on the Dales.

Arthur Raistrick's *Face of North West Yorkshire* is still an excellent introduction to the physical geography of the Dales so my brief was to concentrate on matters human. My teaching interest has moved more and more into the realm of landscape history and this is all too obvious in this book. It is really an attempt to write about some of the aspects of the landscape as it is now so as to understand it better myself. By taking specific places and specific topics it is hoped that ideas that are introduced will lead to the reader enquiring further into those places in which he or she is interested and thereby building from this base with his or her own discoveries.

I am very grateful to Delphine Brown for drawing many of the maps and to my wife for turning my illegible writing into a typed text and to my father Maurice Barringer for allowing me to use one of his drawings. I am also grateful to David Joy for persevering with me over the years and encouraging me to complete this book which has taken far longer than it should have done.

Finally, I must thank John Baker, Assistant National Park Officer of the Yorkshire Dales National Park, for commenting on the final chapter. I, of course, accept responsibility for any errors it and any other chapters may contain.

J. C. Barringer,
Hethersett,
Norfolk.

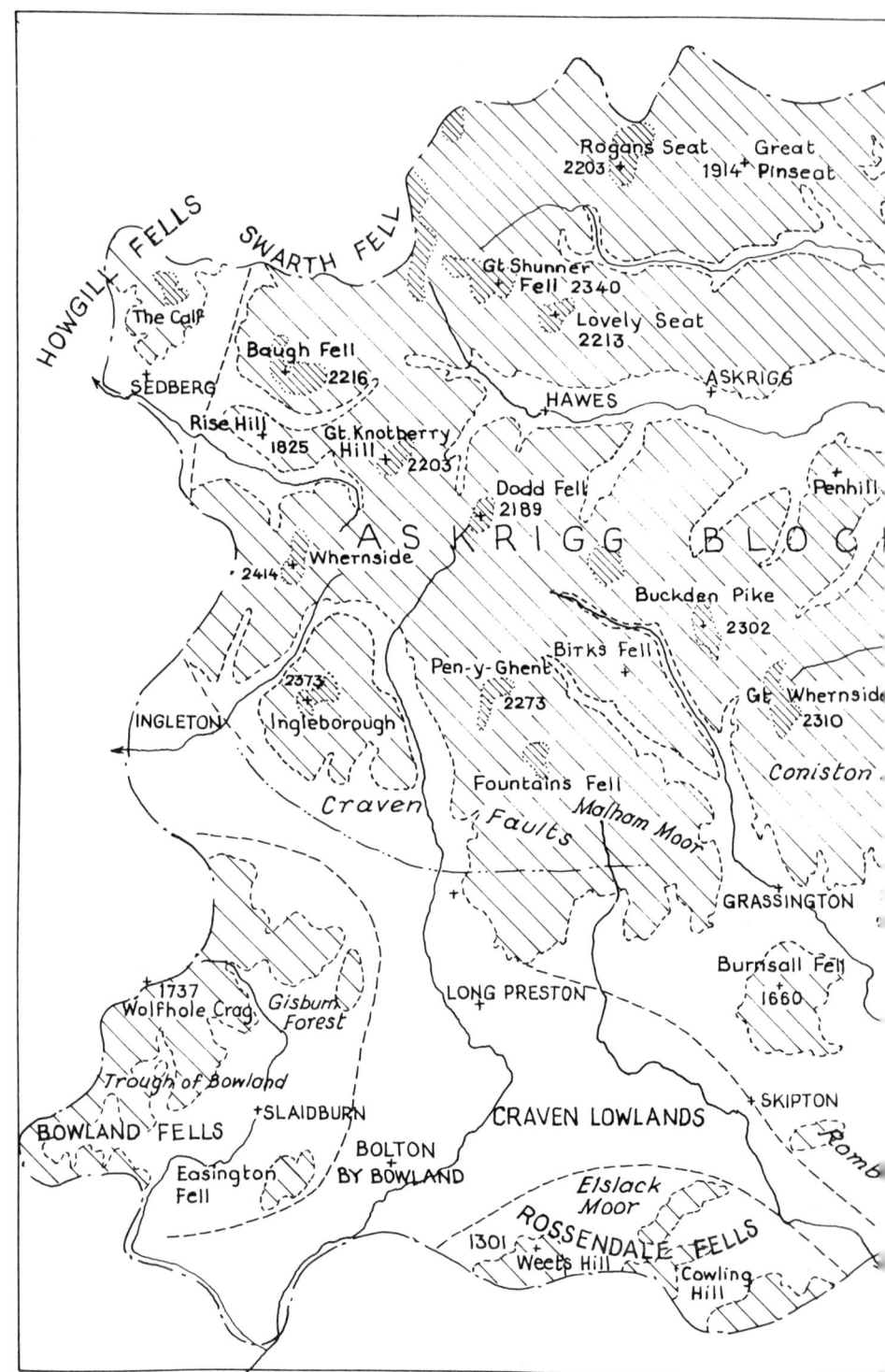

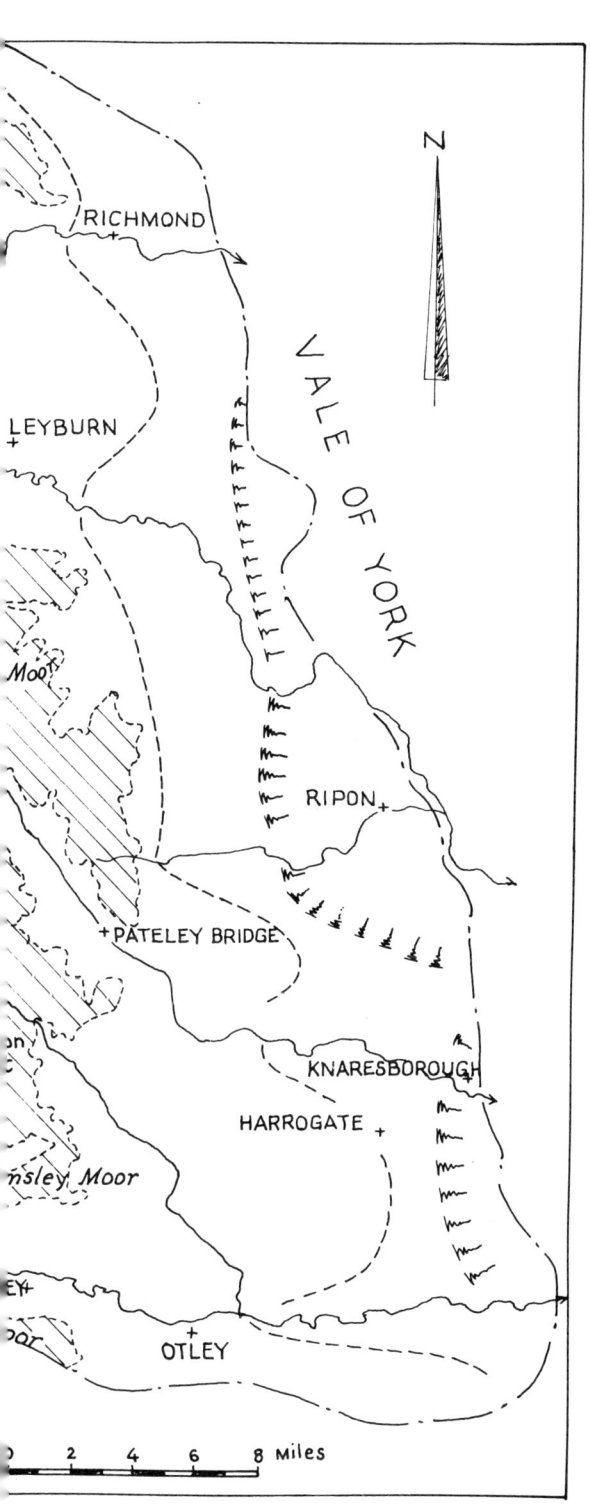

Fig. 1. Relief and drainage.

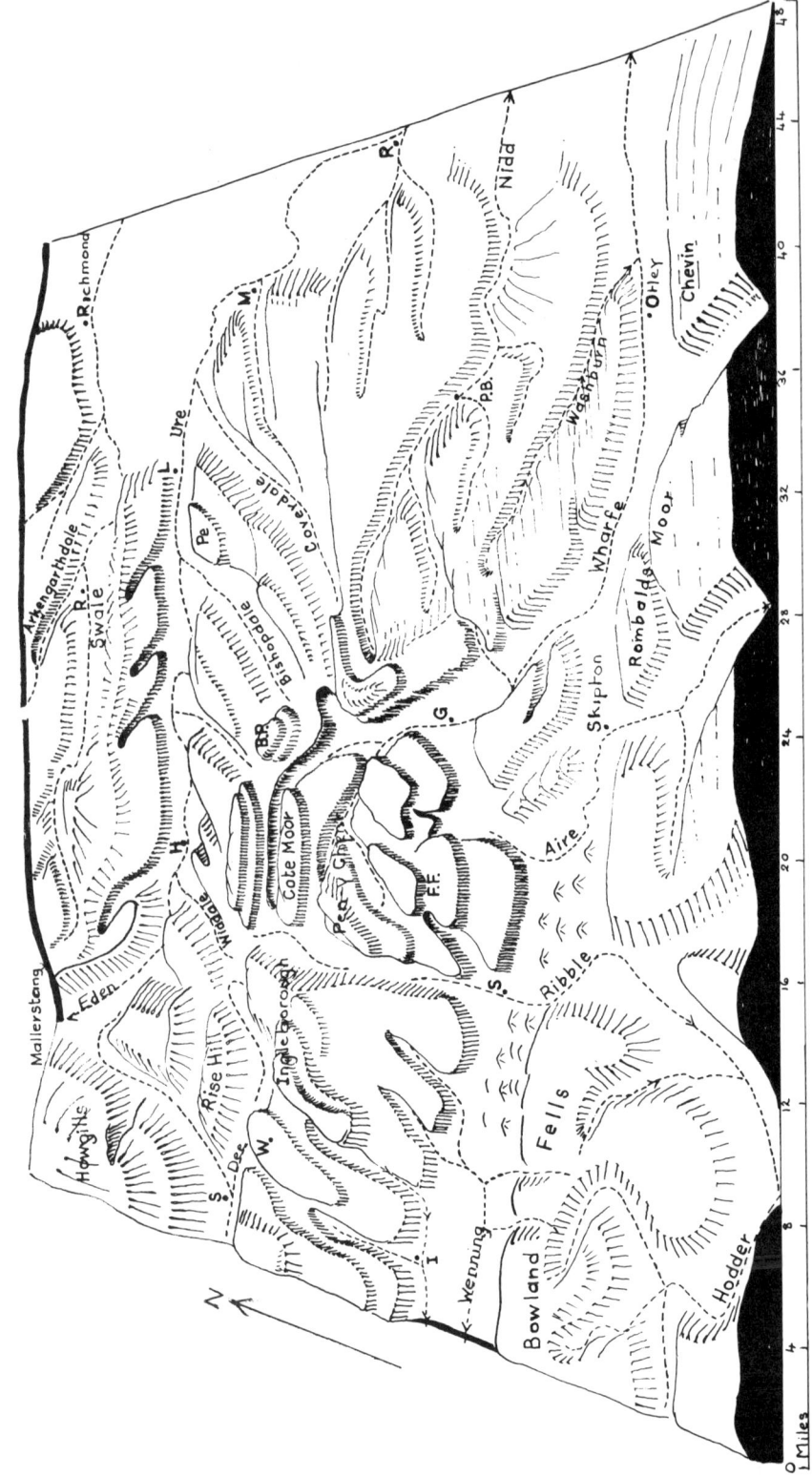

N

Mallerstang
Richmond
Arkengarthdale
R. Swale
Ure
R. Eden
Howgills
Rise Hill
S. Dee
W.
Ingleborough
Middle
Pe
Bishopdale
Coverdale
B.R.
Cote Moor
Penyghent
F.F.
S.
G.
M.
P.B.
R.
Nidd
Washburn
Otley
Chevin
Wharfe
Rombalds Moor
Skipton
Aire
Ribble
Fells
Wenning
I
Bowland
Hodder

0   1 Miles
4
8
12
16
20
24
28
32
36
40
44
48

1
The Land

Its Rocks

The map and the block diagram of the Yorkshire Dales show the major relief units that combine to form the area with which this book is concerned (figs. 1 and 2). Very broadly it lies between the Vale of York to the east and the Lancashire plain to the west. The valley of the River Aire forms the southern boundary and the Stainmore gap sets the northern limit to the region. The major structural element of the region is that known as the Craven or Askrigg block. It gives way south of the Aire Valley to the folded carboniferous rocks of the dome of the southern Pennines and to the west to the same rocks which are domed to form the Forest of Bowland. To the north-west of the faults which bound the Askrigg block on its west side lie the Howgill Fells and the Barbon Fells between the Lune Valley and Dentdale. The whole region is some 45 miles from east to west and some 40 miles from north to south and lies within the areas known until April 1974 as the West Riding and the North Riding of Yorkshire: it is largely within the post-1974 new North Yorkshire and the Forest of Bowland now lies in Lancashire.

The tilted Askrigg block rises high in the west and slopes gently away eastwards. This means that streams such as the Ribble and Dee that flow westwards fall swiftly to the lowlands of Lancashire and drain to the Irish Sea. Those flowing eastwards have a much gentler, longer course that finally leads to their water flowing to the North Sea via the Humber. A network of semi-parallel streams has evolved down this eastern slope—the Swale, Ure, Nidd, Wharfe and Aire. Between the valleys of these rivers there are stretches of plateau which form the moors and fells so typical of the area. The main valleys and their systems of tributary valleys are isolated from one another and it is this physical distinctiveness that makes one so aware of the individuality of each of the dales.

The nature of the rocks on which a landscape forms must always be reflected in the sorts of soil that develop, in the shape of the surface of ground and in the raw materials which they provide for economic activity.

Fig. 2.   Block diagram of the Dales.

Table 1.

The geological sequence in the Dales

ERA	PERIOD	SERIES	Approx. age	Major physical events
Tertiary	Quaternary	Holocene	10000 b.p.	{ Peat formation { river erosion/lake infilling
		Pleistocene	? 3 million	glaciation: erosion/deposition
		Pliocene Miocene Oligocene Eocene Palaeocene	no deposits	erosion Alpine faulting
Secondary	Cretaceous Jurassic Triassic	? ? New Red Sandstones	90 million	erosion desert conditions
Primary	Permian	Magnesium limestones		Hercynian mountains folding: Pennine faults mineral veins (lead)
	Carboniferous Upper	Coal Measures Millstone grits Yoredale/Bowland shales		delta infilling sea muddier sea
	Carboniferous Lower	Great Scar limestone		clear warm sea
		unconformity	250 million	
	Devonian Silurian Ordovician Cambrian	mainly Ludlow Ashgillian/Caradocian	500 million	erosion Caledonian mountains Howgill Fells
Pre Cambrian		Ingletonian		pre-Caledonian folds

Geology has perhaps provided the basic difference between South Yorkshire (in the geographic sense) and the Dales: the existence of coal in South Yorkshire led to the growth of manufacturing industry on a wide scale and this is perhaps the major difference between the two areas. The rock sequence of the Dales is shown in Table 1. Whilst the pre-carboniferous rocks form an important base to the region and indeed give rise to the very interesting area of the Howgill Fells to the north of Sedbergh, they form a relatively small part of the total landscape area. It is the Carboniferous rocks that provide the bulk of the underlying rocks of the area. These beds represent tens of millions of years of growth of muds, sands and shells on the floor of an ancient sea. This sea finally filled in, very much as the

Limestone scenery. **1.** Gaping Ghyll – a major pothole at the junction between the Yoredales and the Great Scar Limestone. **2.** Limestone pavement above Malham Cove. **3.** The stepped valley side of Cowside Beck near Arncliffe, Littondale.

Gulf of Mexico is being filled in by the muds deposited by the Mississippi River today.

The Carboniferous limestone was laid down in a clear, tropical sea and it was formed of myriads of shell, sea lily and coral fragments. It is over five hundred feet thick in places and the susceptibility of limestone to solution by rain water means that systems of shafts or potholes and tunnels or caves have been opened out along the natural vertical joints and horizontal bedding-planes in the rock. In this way such systems as those of Gaping Ghyll (photo 1) and Ingleborough Cave, Stump Cross Caverns near Pateley Bridge and White Scar Cave near Ingleton have been formed. In some areas very distinctive limestone 'pavements' have also been produced by solution: outstanding examples of these formations are to be seen above Malham Cove (photo 2). Steep limestone gorges and valleys cut deeply into the limestone plateaux (photo 3).

Gradually the limestone sea became muddier and a record of a rhythmic pattern of muddy seas followed by clearer water and then a return to muddier conditions has survived in the rocks termed the Yoredale Series (photo 4). The different layers in these beds weather at different rates and provide the distinctive stepped hillsides that are so characteristic of many of the dales (photo 13). In the later stages of the Carboniferous period the sea became muddier still as the rivers flowing into it began to pour in thousands of feet of sands and gravels, bringing them apparently from a land mass located roughly where the Scottish Highlands and Norway now lie. These rough, sandy deposits have become known as the Millstone Grits, because of the great industrial value of some of the coarse gritstone layers within the series. Erosion has almost completely removed these from the high western fells and they survive only as the distinctive cap rocks on the highest hills such as Ingleborough but farther east they form the major landscape element. The rock weathers down into a rather sandy, acid soil and the heather moors are a reflection partly of this underlying rock.

The geological story has two other aspects that are of great importance to the human history of the region. The first is that of the most recent series of geological events known as the Ice Ages. Between a millon and half a million years ago the climate deteriorated over much of north-west Europe: ice caps developed on the high uplands and glaciers flowed away from them down the river valleys. These glaciers deepened and widened the former river valleys to make them more trough-like. They scoured away the soils that had evolved over long periods before the onset of the ice; vegetation and prehistoric man disappeared from the region. The glaciers came and went a number of times until finally they melted about fifteen thousand years ago. As they melted they left dumps of the debris of rock waste which they were carrying. In places this was left as a barrier across a valley floor, as a terminal moraine, in others it was a veneer on the valley floor and sides. Where a moraine lay across the valley floor a lake was held back so that the dales' valleys must have looked very like those of

Rock patterns. **4.** Fine bedding in Yoredale sandstones on Ingleborough. **5.** Slate quarry near Pecca Falls.

6. The Craven Fault, viewed from Settle to the north-west. Ingleborough in the background; limestone pavements in middle distance; lime quarry just to the north of Settle. (Cambridge Univeristy Collection).

the present day Lake District with a number of lakes on their floors and tributary streams building out deltas into them; the lakes disappeared either by being filled in with debris brought down the valley or by a stream cutting down its outlet across the moraine and draining the lake so that the deltas remained as dry sites for settlement. In some areas new channels were cut as at Richmond in Swaledale either by the glaciers or by the vast quantities of meltwater flowing from them. It is likely that the River Ribble may well have flowed to the North Sea before the Ice Age. Steep cliffs such as that of Kilnsey Crag along the flanks of the present-day valleys may well be explained by the fact that a glacier scoured the valley side at that point, some twenty thousand years ago.

The geological history of the area has had its impact on man in terms of the economic value of the rocks and of the minerals which they contain as well as in terms of the scenery to which they give rise. The old hard rocks that form the platform on which the Carboniferous rocks lie provide useful material for road metal. In a few places these old rocks reveal a slatey character sufficient to have made them worth working as a roofing material; a disused quarry in the glens at Ingleton is shown in photo 5. Two slate dealers had businesses in Ingleton in 1822, according to Baines' Directory. The Carboniferous limestone is an important building stone and it provides a chunky material, not easily carved however. The limestones are more important now for their lime content than for their building value. Old lime kilns can be seen in many villages; the heavy rainfall on the western Pennines quickly leaches the lime out of the shallow soil even on the areas of limestone. As transport improved so the national importance of these deposits was recognised and the economies of large scale working made themselves felt: limestone quarries producing agricultural lime and lime for cement now form one of the largest industrial elements in the Dales landscape (photo 6). In economic terms also the very existence of limestone scenery has become a major attraction at sites such as the various caves mentioned and at Malham Cove, Goredale Scar and the Ingleton Glens.

The complex events that have led to the formation of the Pennine 'ranges' and the formation of the system of faults (photo 6), especially down the western edge of the Pennines, has meant that many lines of weakness were created in the Carboniferous rocks. Molten material from the lower layers of the earth's crust was released during the various stages of faulting and folding that have taken place and this material cooled out within the limestones to give mineral veins containing lead ore (galena) and several calcium compounds, the chief of which are calcite, fluorspar and barytes. The existence of these minerals has been very significant in the Grassington, Pateley Bridge and Reeth areas in shaping the landscape as we now see it.

The Yoredale rocks have limestones and sandstones within them (photos 7 and 8) and both small-scale lime workings and lead mining have taken place in the areas where they outcrop. The importance of Millstone Grit has already been stressed for its industrial use but it also provided an extremely valuable building stone and in all areas where it outcrops considerable quarrying has taken place, first for local use and later for national buildings after the railways had been made (see chapter 7). When a change in the nature of the rocks takes place, especially from 'hard' to 'soft', a waterfall may be formed on a stream course. It is at such points that this natural fall can be used by man to power a mill so that again we find the solid geology having an important influence on man's activity. In the gritstone areas, Brimham Rocks, Almscliffe Crag and the Cow and Calf at Ilkley have become tourist attractions either for their curiosity and scenic value or because of the value of the rocks as a training ground for climbers.

There are one or two places where coal outcrops on the surface. On the moors between Wensleydale and Swaledale thin coal seams existed within the Yoredales and these gave rise to surface coal pits. At Ingleton the downthrow of the Craven Fault preserved a small area of the coal measures and a colliery functioned there into the early years of the twentieth century.

The glacial geology, mainly in the form of glacial deposits, is very varied within the Dales. It can be seen to have considerable importance between Otley and Ilkley on the Wharfe where there are large gravel workings into the glacial and post-glacial infill of the flood plain of the present River Wharfe. Most parishes had at least one gravel pit cut into the glacial or fluvio-glacial deposits. The coarse nature of the gravels has meant that stone has been a better source of building material than any local clay; brick building has thus been a feature only of the nineteenth century in most of the Dales and indeed it is discouraged by the National Park planners at least as a facing material even now. Small pockets of glacial clay and of Coal Measures clay have been worked occasionally— for example there was a pottery at Burton in Lonsdale: in 1822 John Bates was making earthern-ware there.

The Regions

The major subdivisions of the area under consideration are shown in fig. 5. The Howgill Fells shown on fig. 3 form a distinctive and dramatic area standing high to the north of Sedbergh. The Calf is only 2,220 feet high but from all directions the ascent is steep and a system of deep, steep-sided streams has dissected the ancient rocks of this massif to give a very attractive and varied landscape (photo 7). The steep hills are grass covered without the typical plateau peat bogs of the Pennines proper. Because they stand so isolated the views from their ridges and summits in every direction are especially fine.

The major area of the Dales consists, as has been pointed out, of a massive plateau of Carboniferous rocks tilted eastwards towards the Plain of York. It is worth distinguishing between the limestone zone and the gritstone zone of this area as being the extremes: the Yoredales in places contribute their own distinctive character between the two major elements. The limestone zone has four major characteristics: the limestone strata show through' the grass cover to give a horizontal grain to the landscape. This is well shown in photos 6 and 9. The intensive grazing of stock on

7. The Howgills—the head of Langdale looking south from West Fell to the Calf. Fig. 3. The Howgill Fells.

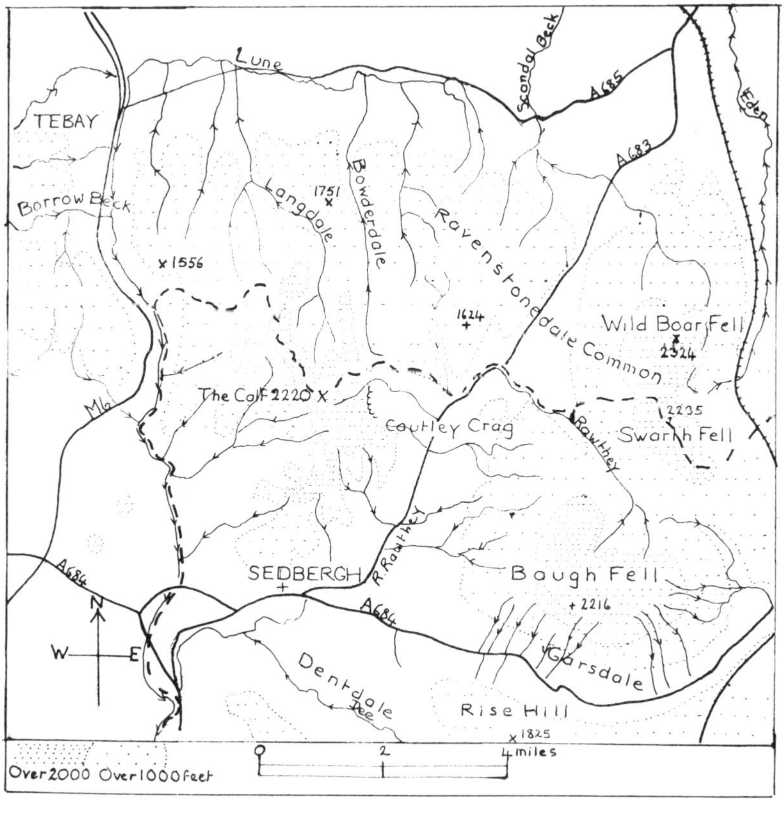

Over 2000 Over 1000 feet

The map labels:
- Lune
- Scandal Beck
- A685
- Eden
- TEBAY
- A683
- Borrow Beck
- Langdale
- Bowderdale
- Ravenstonedale Common
- 1751 ×
- × 1556
- 1624 +
- Wild Boar Fell
- 2324 ×
- The Calf 2220 ×
- M6
- Cautley Crag
- Rawthey
- 2235
- Swarth Fell
- A684
- N
- W — E
- SEDBERGH +
- R Rawthey
- A684
- Baugh Fell
- + 2216
- Garsdale
- Dentdale
- Dee
- Rise Hill
- × 1825
- 0   2   4 miles

the rich grass has made the limestone zone largely treeless except on very steep slopes where indigenous ash wood may have survived. Bracken and heather rarely add their browns and purples to the landscape so that limestone country is always far greener than that of the gritstones. Finally the intricate pattern of stone walling is especially striking on the limestones with the light limestone contrasting with the greens of the pastures and rough grazing.

The gritstone moors tend to be more continuous than the limestone areas, the more massive grits form very distinctive edges to the moors but the shales weather to give less stepped slopes than those of the limestones. The acid nature of the soils produced from the sandy grit gives rise to much wider expanses of bracken and heather moor than occurs on the limestones. The flatter summits and the less porous debris on them favour the development of more peat bog on the grits than on the limestones. The landscape is darker and browner than that of the limestones but it changes more with the seasons than does that of the limestones. The long gritstone walls do not stand out as sharply as those made out of limestone (photos 8 and 10).

On the limestones, the farmstead shows up clearly amongst its pattern

8 (below). Gritstone moors: acid soils and heather. Roundhill reservoir from High Ash Head Moor— the view east from the Askrigg Block out to the Plain of York. 9 (opposite). Peaks, pavements and valleys—Penyghent from Crummockdale. (photo: Cambridge University Collection).

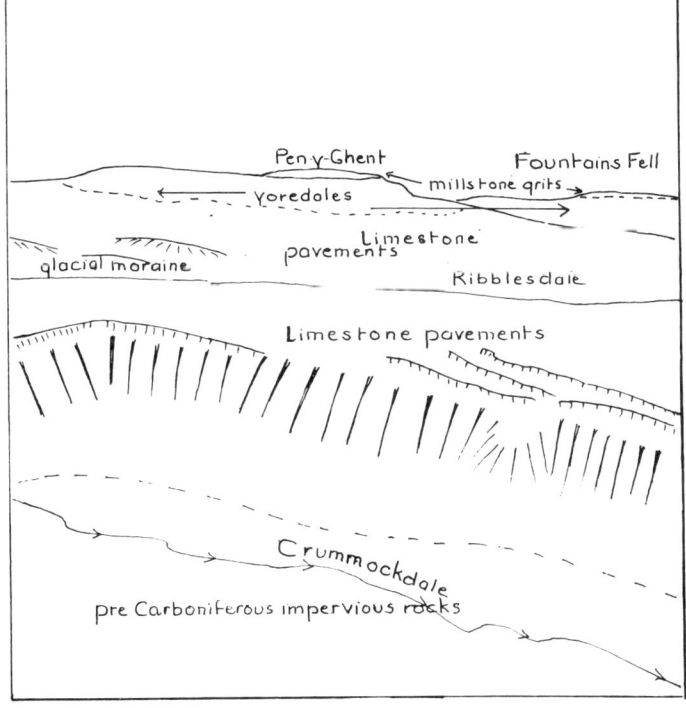

Pen-y-Ghent   Fountains Fell

millstone grits

Yoredales

Limestone
pavements

glacial moraine   Ribblesdale

Limestone pavements

Crummockdale

pre Carboniferous impervious rocks

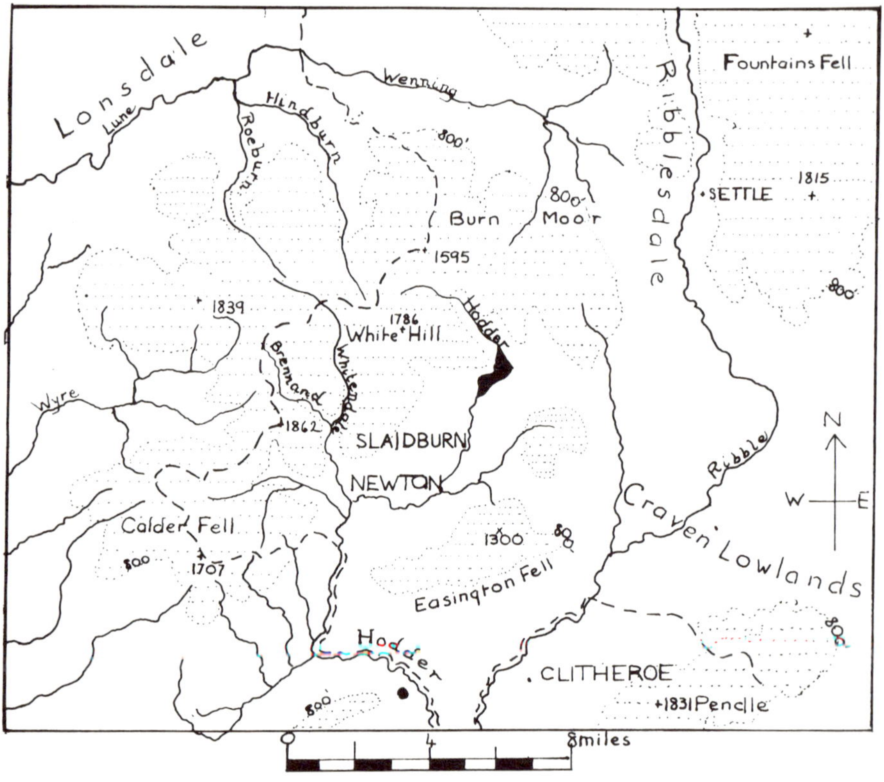

Lonsdale

Lume

Roeburn

Hindburn

Wenning

800'

800'
Moor

Burn

+1595

Ribblesdale

Fountains Fell

+

SETTLE
+1815
+

800

+1839

White Hill
1786

Hodder

Bremand

Whitendale

+1862

SLAIDBURN

NEWTON

Wyre

Calder Fell

800
+1707

1300

Easington Fell

800

Hodder

800

Ribble

Craven Lowlands

800

CLITHEROE

+1831 Pendle

N

W   E

8miles
4

of small stone enclosures and it is often protected by half a dozen windblown sycamore trees. The landscape of the Yoredales has many of the elements mentioned already. The alternation of limestones, shales and sandstones does give rise to a marked steplike nature of hillsides where they outcrop; this is nowhere seen better than on the Three Peaks where the contrast between limestone country on their lower slopes, Yoredales on the upper and Millstone Grits on their summits is very marked.

The third area, that of the Craven Lowlands, contrasts markedly with the previous area of the Dales proper. These lowlands occupy a triangle bounded by the Craven faults to the east, the Trough of Bowland to the north-west, and the Rossendale Forest to the south-west. The extended apex of the triangle points westwards down the Ribble Valley. The detailed relief of these lowlands stems almost entirely from the last stages of the glaciations when masses of hummocky boulder clay were deposited as swarms of drumlins. The rivers Aire and Ribble twist across this lowland and the damp heavy soils with badly drained pockets of lowland between the mounds produce rich grass so that this is a dairy and beef farming area par excellence. Skipton, Gargrave, Long Preston, Settle and Gisburn fringe it as markets between this lowland and the uplands behind them.

The Forest of Bowland is the fourth distinctive area (fig. 4). Clearly defined physically it now all lies in Lancashire but part of it was included in the study on historical grounds that it lay within the ancient Deanery of Craven. Bowland Forest is the Pennines writ small in geological terms: geologically it can be viewed as a dome, deeply dissected by the tributaries of the Hodder flowing to the south and those of the Lune flowing to the north. In the centre of the area the limestones give rise to the characteristic scenery described above. There is also some evidence of lead mining. The Bowland Shales, the equivalent of the Yoredale Shales (see table 1), form a ring around the limestones and the Millstone Grits in turn stand high above them. It is a region of deep and attractive valleys in which scattered farms are concealed, and between which stretch wide sweeps of grouse moor (photo 10).

Only a north-eastern fringe of Rossendale Forest comes within our area, again because of historical ties, but it is a region now in many ways much more closely linked with the industrial areas of West Yorkshire (1974 Metropolitan County).

Finally in the east of the region the Dales give way to the Plain of York. As the last chapter in the book discusses, various degrees of importance have been acknowledged in attempting to assess the relative merits of landscape within the total area of this study. A proposed green belt lies along

10. Forest of Bowland: the Brennand valley looking west from near Brennand House.   Fig. 4. The Forest of Bowland.

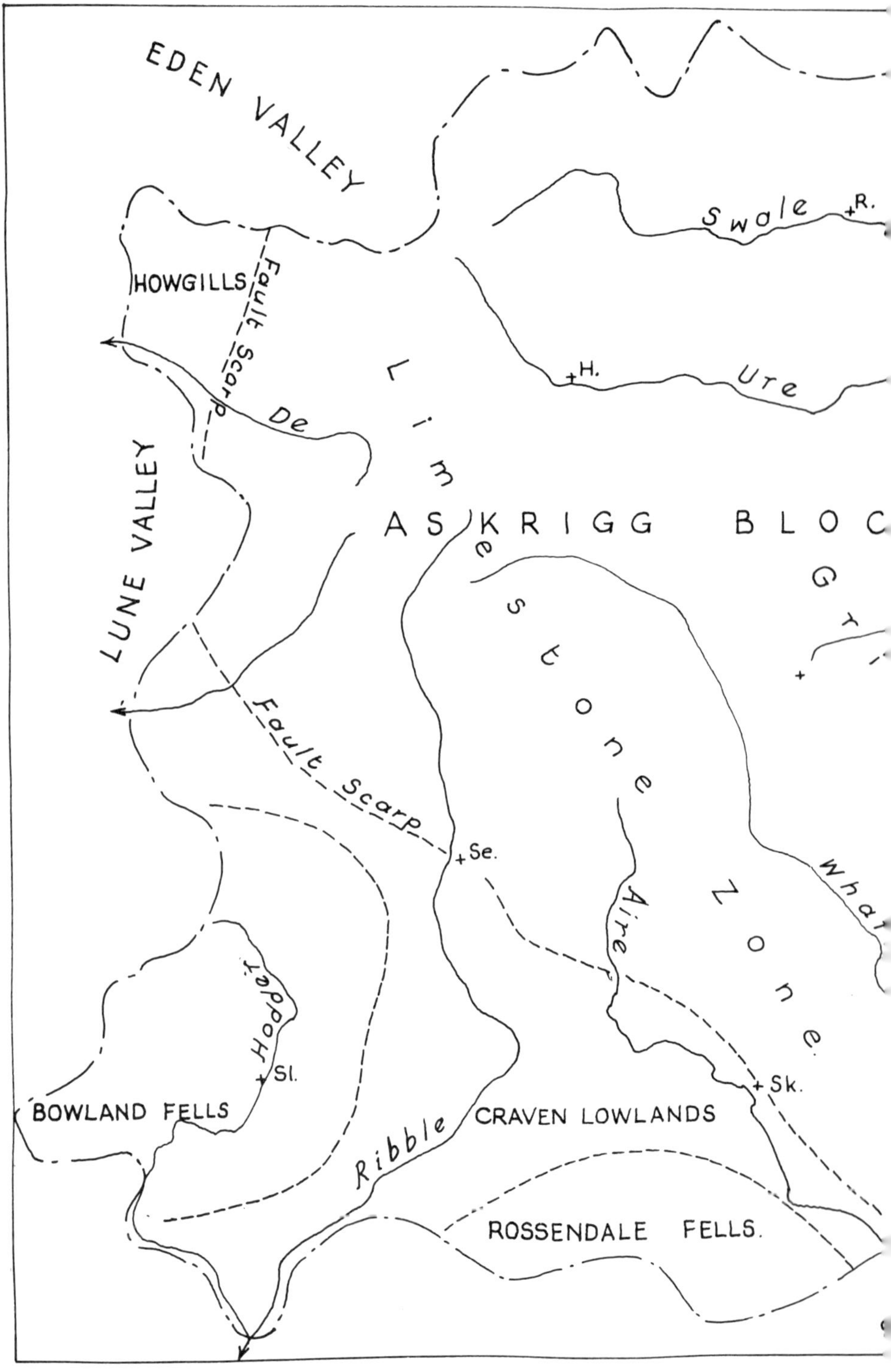

EDEN VALLEY

Swale

+R.

HOWGILLS

Fault Scarp De

+H.

Ure

LUNE VALLEY

L i m e s t o n e   Z o n e

A S K R I G G   B L O C

G r i

+

Fault Scarp

+Se.

Aire

Wha

Hodder

Sl.

+Sk.

BOWLAND FELLS

CRAVEN LOWLANDS

Ribble

ROSSENDALE   FELLS.

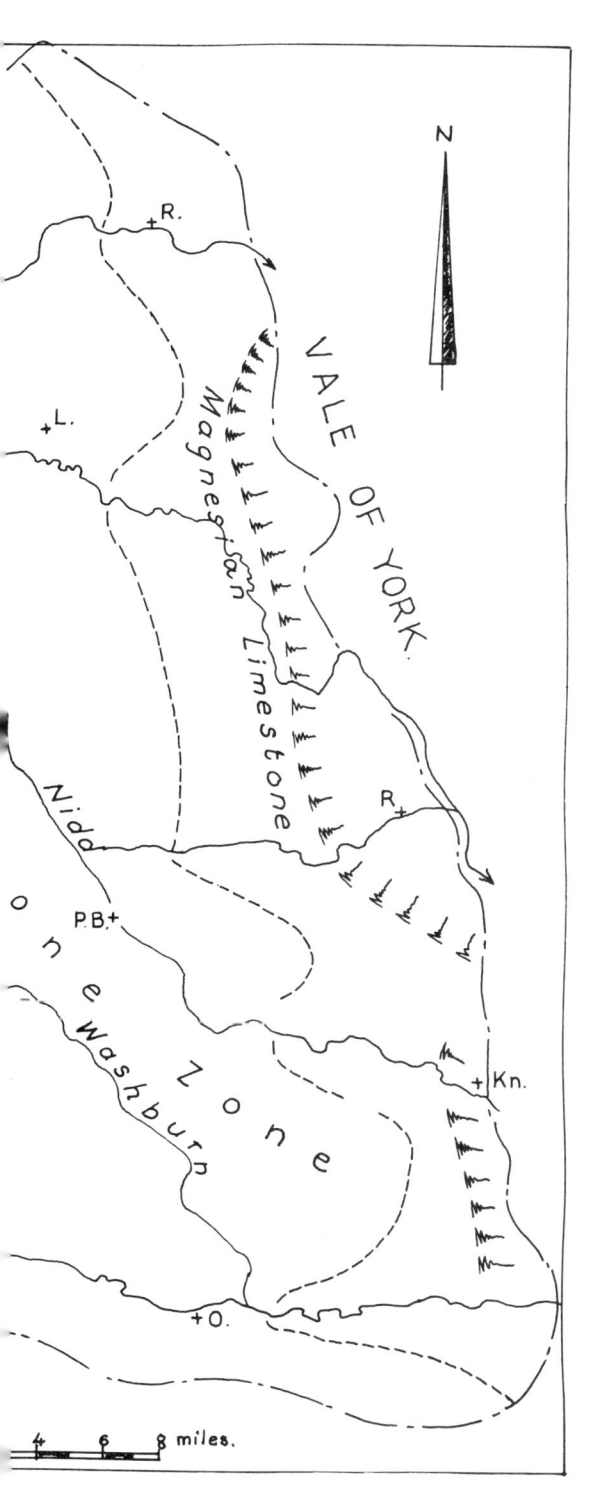

Fig. 5.   Regions of the Dales.

this western fringe of the Vale. As the maps suggest, the Vale of York can be seen as spreading its fingers up the valleys well into the Dales. Otley, Ripon and Masham are in many ways upper limits of the Vale but they are tied in also as markets to the uplands: very simply hill sheep and cattle meet lowland wheat and barley at markets such as these. They are classic market points at the junction between upland and lowland.

The Climate

The climate of the Dales, or perhaps more correctly the climates of the Dales, are of great importance in influencing the way in which man can live within the area. Table 2 shows that rainfall decreases from west to east and that it increases with height. The range of climates combines with the many different solid rock and drift surfaces to produce a very wide range of habitats for plant growth.

The broad control exercised by the climate on human activity is to make the higher areas less attractive to food producers and therefore to settlement. Land over about 1000 feet is usually too cool and too wet for crops to ripen on it. Highest levels for hay making vary with soil type, aspect and farming skills. New techniques such as silage making also increase the height at which it may be worth growing hay: indeed recent price increases will almost certainly encourage farmers to push their cereal and hay limits higher than was economic in a period of low world prices. It would be a very interesting exercise for a school or college to keep careful record of such changes in their own localities. If we select places between 250ft and

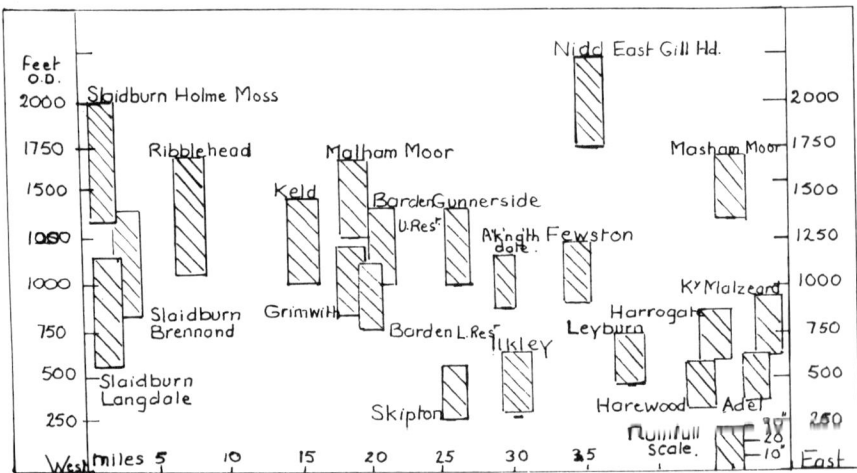

Table 2. Rainfall plotted against height and position from west to east.

500ft and join their precipitation columns together and those of 1,250ft and 1,500ft together we achieve a visual impression of the decrease in rainfall from west to east. Also, if we take places at the same distance on the east-west scale we see that height too is important, e.g. Nidderdale and Harewood. Giggleswick and Harrogate are within a hundred feet of one another in height: their mean annual temperatures are 9.0°C (48.3°F) and 9.3°C (48.7°F) respectively—surprisingly January is just a little colder at Giggleswick than at Harrogate. The July mean of Harrogate is one degree higher than that for Giggleswick as might be expected. Their climates however are to a large extent similar as far as their temperatures are concerned. In terms of extremes of temperature it is clear that the eastern side of the Pennines is more likely to have more really hot days than the west in summer; on the other hand and perhaps surprisingly Giggleswick had a much lower January extreme than has been recorded at Harrogate.

The natural vegetation of the Dales

It might perhaps be more accurate to term this section the vegetation of the Dales because it is becoming increasingly clear that there are virtually no habitats, perhaps other than cliff faces and the sides of potholes, where man and/or his animals have not had some effect on the plant and soil cover that has evolved over the bed-rocks and glacial deposits.

The classic study of the vegetation of Yorkshire was made by Smith and Rankin in the Geographical Journal of 1903. The New Naturalist volume

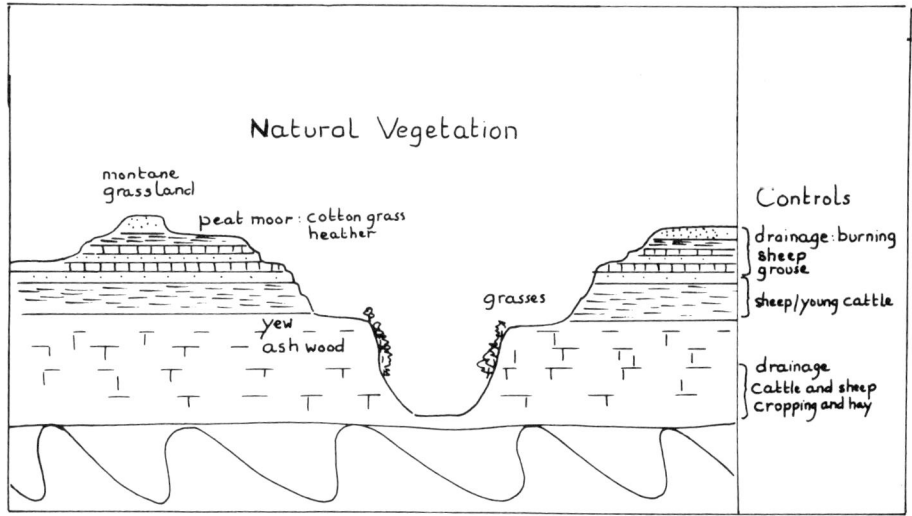

Fig. 6.   Natural vegetation of the Dales.

The sequence of vegetation in the Dales from summit to valley floor. **11.** Moor top – a near Arctic climate with peat erosion. **12.** Peat bog on the gritstone. **13.** Upper pastures on the Yoredale Series. **14.** Ash and thorn wood on the Great Scar Limestone. **15.** Valley floor – meadows, alder and ash hedgerows.

by Pearsall on *Mountains and Moorland* has also a great deal of relevant material in it. Raistrick's *Face of North West Yorkshire* has a relevant section too. What have the various vegetation types meant to man in the Dales? To what extent have they affected human activity? It is perhaps easiest to start with the high gritstone moors and work downslope in considering such a question.

The gritstone moors of the Pennines tend to have a tabular form with badly drained plateaux (photos 11 and 12). Acid peat bogs occur over wide stretches of these moors, the dominant plants being cotton-grass, cross-leaved heath, sphagnum, bilberry, heather and crowberry. On the dryer soils and gentle slopes heather moor becomes dominant and on the steepest slopes bilberry take over. These stretches of moor separate the townships and parish boundaries tend to follow the watersheds between the valleys. Each township therefore had a stretch of moor within its bounds and apart from its value for extensive summer grazing its great value was as a source of peat. The peat was cut in the summer and a graded track invariably leads from each township up on to the moor. Sledges may have been used until relatively recently for carrying down peat and also perhaps bracken for bedding for stock. Rights of turberry (turf/peat cutting) were important common rights to the people of all Dales townships. The outcrops of gritstone between plateaux may well have meant that it was quarried from the sixteenth century onwards for building stone and in a few sites for millstones.

Over much of the Dales a zone of limestones occurs below the gritstone moors. These are localised within the Yoredales Series outcrop but much more widespread where the Mountain Limestone occurs. The 'natural' vegetation of the limestone has virtually disappeared as a result of several thousand years of grazing by stock and phases of cultivation by men. The most typical element of 'natural' vegetation of the limestones is perhaps that of the ashwood (photo 14). These woods occur most frequently on areas of limestone pavement and craggy hillsides where stock cannot easily graze. Bartley in *Leeds and its Regions* points out that recent work is leading to the conclusion that such areas were probably originally covered with oak/elm forest and that ash is from secondary woodland.

In the limestone clints (the gaps in pavements) and on the limestone crags specialised calcifuges are to be found such as the saxifrages, but in the main the limestones support grasses that make a good grazing sward so that millennia of grazing have produced limestone pastures and meadows when woodland would otherwise flourish. Limestone gorges where

16. The natural landscape – Bowderdale in the Howgill Fells.   **17.** Man and nature – above Conistone in Wharfedale.   **18.** Man controlling nature – limestone walls and sycamore trees, Malham.

stock cannot easily graze do offer distinctive and very interesting habitats. On the lower valley slopes and the valley bottoms woodland would be the natural vegetation but there are relatively few areas where any survives.

The final three photographs in this chapter (photos 16–18) are the links between this introduction to the 'natural' landscape and the landscape that man has shaped over several thousand years. Bowderdale (fig. 3) in the Howgill Fells shows natural processes at work. A glaciated trough valley is being modified by stream erosion: a former marsh or perhaps tarn site is being encroached upon by the scree, hill wash and alluvial remnants from the ancient rocks, which make up the Howgills. Whilst man has almost certainly built sheepfolds and summer huts in these valleys the human impact is minimal. Only the grazing of sheep has altered the natural pattern of vegetation which would almost certainly be alder carr and some oak in the valley bottom with birch scrub up the lower slopes.

Above Coniston in Wharfedale, snow has picked out the finer texture of the hillsides. The same processes of stream erosion and hillside debris movement are at work as in the Howgill Fells but hillside tracks and terracettes, made in part by stock, are also obvious. Stone walls, a derelict barn, sycamore trees and improved pasture show that man has had a greater impact here. The derelict barn emphasises that what may make agricultural sense at one time may not suit new circumstances.

The third photograph showing the complex wall systems below Malham Cove illustrates a more complete control of nature by man. This wall system probably combines Celtic elements as well as survivals from the medieval strips, both of which still show through in the present alignment and density of walls. Such a network would not have survived the new agricultural revolutions had this not been an area of stock farming rather than arable farming. The Pennine Way sign also emphasises the new 'leisure' use which the majority of the population see the countryside as having, rather than the few who live and work in it.

Succeeding chapters look in more detail at the way in which man has altered the 'natural' landscape.

References
This chapter is in no way an exhaustive study of the physical geography of the Dales. The following are some of the main texts covering the various aspects of their physical geography and each contains further references.
A. Raistrick and J. Illingworth, *The Face of North West Yorkshire*, Dalesman 1967.
A. Raistrick, *The Ice Age in Yorkshire*, Dalesman 1968.
D. A. Wray, *The Pennines and Adjacent Areas*, H.M.S.O., various editions.
Cuchlaine A. M. King, *Northern England (Geomorphology)*, Methuen 1976.
M W. Beresford and G. R. J. Jones, *Leeds and its Region*, B.A.A.S., Leeds 1967, Chs. 1–5.
Cuchlaine A. M. King, *The Yorkshire Dales*, Geographical Association, 1960.

2
The Story of Settlement
Neolithic Colonisation to the Norman Conquest

THIS is not intended to be a detailed account of the prehistory of the Yorkshire Dales but in looking at the patterns of farms, hamlets, villages and market towns that we see today it must always be of interest to try to understand something of the way in which the present day settlement pattern has come into existence. Is it the characteristics of a people or is it the nature of the land that they settle that determines the form of their settlement pattern? These are interesting and difficult questions: clearly it is far less easy for a community in hill country to develop a system of arable fields around its settlement than for one in a lowland area. The linear nature of the valleys and the varied slopes of the valley sides impose limits on the possibilities of farming the land in upland areas.

Mesolithic 8000 B.C.—2500 B.C.
The later stages of the melting of the ice sheets and glaciers, some 10,000–15,000 years ago, saw Palaeolithic and then later Mesolithic Man wandering across the southern edge of the area which was soon to become the North Sea. These hunters and gatherers had sophisticated spears, arrows and axes all made of beautifully flaked flint. They caught fish in the rivers and lakes and hunted reindeer as they moved along the gravel terraces of the river valleys and along the glacial moraines: gradually they travelled further and further into the more isolated areas of the hills of north-west Britain. The finds most typical of the Mesolithic people were the very small flints, scrapers and tools termed microliths. Many sites rich in these small flints have been found in the Rombalds Moor area between Wharfedale and Airedale.[1]

Neolithic (3500 B.C.—1500 B.C.)
New Stone Age (Neolithic) Man began to arrive in the Dales from the east perhaps five thousand years ago. These people with their techniques of herding animals and growing crops reached the British Isles about 4000 B.C. The difficulties of the hill country may have discouraged them for some time after this. There are few outstanding Neolithic Sites in the Yorkshire Dales: the Megalithic monuments so typical of the west coast

of Great Britain and inland on Salisbury Plain are few. Two chambered long cairns have been found on Bradley Moor and another at Grimes Grave on Penyghent.

The Beaker phase of the Neolithic is hardly represented in the region and the main Neolithic remains are those of polished axe heads. Langdale axes are the most frequently found, but others have turned up: for example one from Ulster has been found on Blubberhouses Moor, north of Ilkley. This sparse evidence compared with the rather wider finds of Mesolithic material suggests that the Mesolithic hunter probably roamed the Dales to hunt deer and wild boar well into the Neolithic period. The Neolithic axe finds remind us, however, that man already had the capacity to begin to clear the forests that had grown in the valleys and high up onto the hillsides in the ten thousand years after the last glaciers melted.

The Bronze Age (2000 B.C.—500 B.C.)

The use of bronze gave an advantage to those skilled in making it for hunting, fighting and for felling timber. Raistrick has suggested that the physical geography of the Vale of York exercised an important control on the route followed by Bronze Age settlers.[2] Their remains, in particular

19. Cup and ring stone, Green Crag Slack, Ilkley Moor.

axe heads, pottery and stone circles, are spread more densely over the Yorkshire Wolds and the Vale of Pickering than in the Dales. He argued that the Bronze Age invaders used the Escrick and York moraines as their main routes across the forested and marshy Vale of York. This route led them to the lower Wharfe Valley and so to the Rombalds Moor area in particular: other groups moved up Wensleydale and up the east side of the Vale of York along the Pennine foothills. Two rather different areas of Bronze Age settlement are worth discussing in order to see how different physical environments and perhaps different Bronze Age cultures interacted with one another.

At Thornborough, just outside the Dales area, five miles north-west of Ripon, there is an important group of three great henge circles. These are on a massive scale of between 550 and 600 feet in diameter and they are aligned as a group on a north west–south east alignment. Underneath them is an earlier avenue (cursus) on two parallel ditches some 4,000 feet in length.[3] There is another henge in the same area at Nunwick. Features of this scale, whatever their function, imply considerable social organisation and presumably a sizeable population and therefore in turn suggest further forest clearance and spread of agriculture, additional to that accomplished by Neolithic Man.

On Rombalds Moor, stone circles of a type different from those at Thornborough are found at several places: for example, the Twelve Apostles on the Dick Hudson's path—this circle consists of a low bank on which stand the twelve stones, the diameter being only about 50 feet. Perhaps better known and more intriguing than the stone circles are the carved 'cup and ring' stones which occur all along the north facing edge of Rombalds Moor on the exposed masses of millstone grit.[4] Further clusters of cup and ring stones (photo 19) occur on Snowdon Moor, overlooking the Washburn Valley and on the Chevin above Otley, overlooking the Wharfe. The most famous stone of all is the 'Swastika Stone' just to the west of Hebers Ghyll about two miles west of the centre of Ilkley. A question for those interested in the overall settlement of the area is why should Bronze Age Man have found these bleak, infertile gritstone moors so attractive? In all probability, the climate of 1500 B.C. was more pleasant than that of today, almost certainly drier and perhaps warmer. The Wharfe and Aire valleys may well have been filled with forest and had very wet floors. Did wood-using people live in these valleys and merely carve stones in situ for some form of ritual? Do we visualise Bronze Age shepherds and cowherds grazing their stock and growing some crops where bracken and heath now dominate? None of these questions has easy answers, but Cowling's suggestion that a routeway followed this gritstone plateau, from which views were good, and along which woodland was sparse or non-existent is reasonable.[5] Whatever the other aspects of their life were like, it seems that these peoples who made the great circles at Thornborough and carved the stones on Rombald's Moor had considerable powers of organisation and, to judge by the patterns of their carvings, were open to influences from as far away as the Classical World of the Mediterranean.[6]

The Iron Age (750 B.C.—43 A.D.)

The Iron Age had barely begun in much of upland Britain when the Romans arrived. This last stage of prehistoric settlement, not surprisingly, has left us more evidence on the face of the countryside than the earlier phases. The use of iron for axes and for ploughs, meant that the new groups of invaders could undertake more clearance than the Neolithic and Bronze Age peoples had achieved. In the period preceding the Roman conquest, the Iron Age peoples developed sufficient cohesion to group into tribes or even kingdoms.

The kingdom of the Brigantes was the largest of these Celtic states. It is thought to have stretched from the Southern Uplands of Scotland as far south as the line of the rivers Trent and Mersey and from the west coast of Cumbria and Lancashire to the mouths of the Tees and Tyne. The Parisii, another Celtic tribe, controlled the area of Yorkshire which was later to become known as the East Riding.[7] Ptolemy, the Roman geographer, listed nine Brigantian towns of which two, Epiacum and Calatum, have not been placed with any certainty. Fig. 7 shows some of these Brigantian towns which apart from Ingleborough and Stanwick, also became important Roman fort sites.

An outstanding Brigantian site was excavated by Sir Mortimer Wheeler at Stanwick.[9, 10] It began as a hill fort with an area of seventeen acres on a low hill with additional ramparts of 24ft. in height; then an enclosure with earthworks two miles in length, parts of which were cut out of solid rock, was added to the north in A.D. 50–60; finally a third stage enclosing 600 acres with a bank $3\frac{1}{2}$ miles long was built, its main gateway never being completed. Wheeler suggested that Stanwick was the fort of Ventios, leader of the Brigantes against the 9th Spanish legion of Petillius Cerialis, Governor of Britain A.D. 71–74, who attacked from Lincoln. In 1844, a farmer found a hoard of 90 Iron Age objects at Stanwick: these ranged from harnesses to iron hoops from wheels, and are of 1st Century A.D. native workmanship. These finds support the idea that a very important chieftain occupied the site. The fort on the summit of Ingleborough is the outstanding hill fort within the Dales.[11] Other major nearby fort sites were at Almondbury, near Huddersfield, and at Castle Steads near Gayles, between Richmond and Barnard Castle. Cowling, in detailed field mapping in Mid-Wharfedale, notes many smaller banked sites such as that at Bank Slack on the north side of the Washburn Valley, a mile east of Fewston church. He suggests that this was one of a line of defensive Brigantian forts erected to check the Roman advance.[12]

So much for the military aspects of Brigantian life. What then was the nature of this region under Roman military control; where and how did the Iron Age, Celtic population belonging to the Brigantian kingdom live?

The Celtic field systems of the Dales have been studied in particular in the Grassington and Malham areas (photo 20) by Raistrick.[13, 14] Further systems existed in Wensleydale, on Addleborough and Penhill for example. These complexes of small enclosures were bounded by stone banks and contained round huts of about fifteen feet in diameter. The inference to be drawn from the archaeological evidence is that Iron Age peoples occupied many of the limestone plateaux above the main valley floors and that they were agriculturalists to the extent of growing crops of oats and perhaps rye in their small enclosures. The querns that the Brigantes used for grinding their cereals have been found in considerable quantities in Wharfedale, especially at Otley[15], and King found a dozen millstone grit querns at a settlement at Helwith Bridge near Settle[16].

At Stanwick, however, large quantities of bones were revealed during the excavation of the ditches. The bones were 40% those of cattle, 23% of sheep and goats, 16% of pig and 13% of horses: barely 1% were those of deer or hare. This evidence together with the deficiency of quernstones— one only was found at Stanfield, compared with 56 from a similar area at Maiden Castle in Dorset—and a deficiency of grain storage pits, combine to

20. The Celtic field system below Malham Cove, looking south from the Cove.

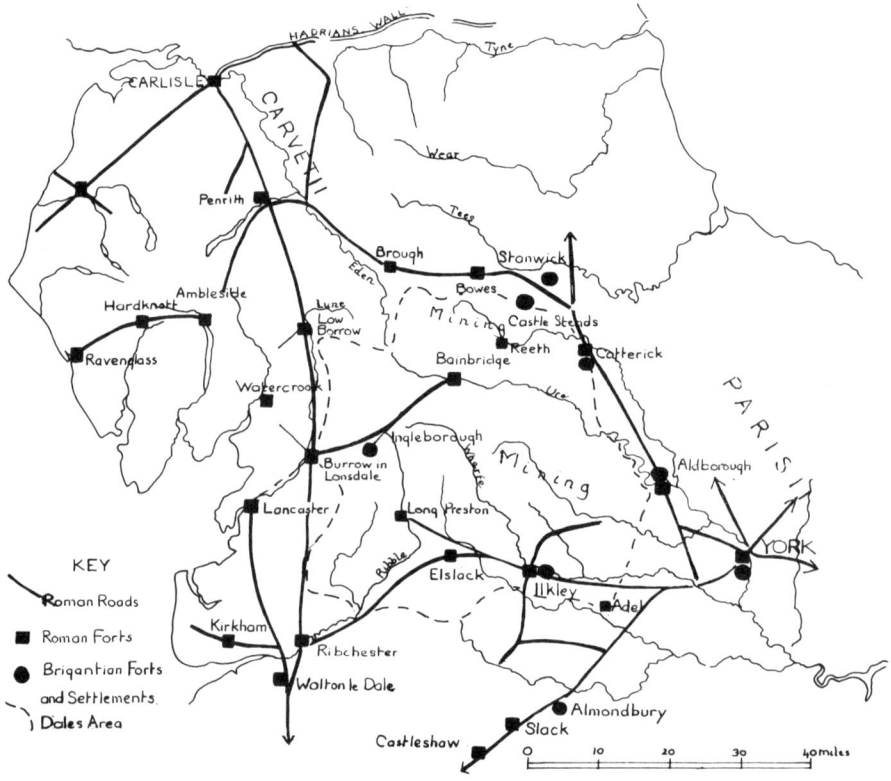

Fig. 7. North-West England: Iron Age and Roman features (based on Margary, Fig. 3, and Hartley, Fig. 1).

suggest that these peoples were largely pastoralists.[17] Their small enclosures near their huts may have been crop growing areas, but most of their territory must have been used for grazing stock. The grazing of hillsides would of course, hold back tree growth and in the case of goats severely inhibit it, so maintaining the clearance of the woodlands and perhaps increasing it in some areas.

The Romans

The Romans in occupying Northern England, faced the problem of the subjugation of the Brigantes who had the advantage of living in the hill country of the Pennines. The major Roman effort was made first under the leadership of Petillius Cerialis, governor of Britain between 74 and

77 A.D. and then of Agricola between 77 and 85 A.D. These two were governors under the emperors of the Flavian family: Vespasian, Titus and Domitian. The legion used by Petillius Cerialis was the IX Spanish legion, based on York, and it defeated a Brigantian force at Stanwick in 74 A.D.

Archaeological evidence is that the first forts, such as those at Ilkley, Bainbridge and Elslack, had earthbanks and ditches and timber buildings and date from Agricola's time.[18, 19] In order to control an otherwise almost inaccessible area the Romans constructed their main routes up the east and west sides of the Pennines and then made cross routes, one using the Wharfe–Aire gap and a second diagonal route linking Burrow-in-Lonsdale with Bainbridge. The modern network of the A1, M6 and A65/A59 from Skipton westwards reflects the three basic routes that the Romans initially established.

After the construction of the wall from the Tyne to the Solway by Hadrian (Emperor 117–138 A.D.) some of the Yorkshire forts may have been left derelict. However, fresh uprisings by the Brigantes led to various stages of reconstruction and modification. Hartley has shown that there were at least four stages of rebuilding after the original construction of the fort at Ilkley and a complex sequence of rebuilding is also being revealed at Bainbridge.

Fig. 7 shows the main Roman roads of the north-west of England and it is based on Margary's map in the second volume of his *Roman Roads in Britain*.[20] The Romans must always have had a particular interest in the Pateley Bridge–Greenhow and Reeth areas as two important lead mining districts. The discovery of pigs of lead with Roman inscriptions has confirmed their activities in these two areas.

Whilst the Romans had established firm military control on the Dales by their network of forts and roads there is relatively little evidence that they managed to Romanise the country to the extent which they must have done around York or even more markedly, in areas further south in England, such as East Anglia. Roman villas have been found at Gargrave, four miles west of Skipton, and at Well, two miles north-east of Masham. A hypocaust provides evidence of a house site having existed at Middleham in Wensleydale. At Aldborough, probably the capital of the Brigantes in the 1st century A.D., the major Roman town of Isurium existed. It was a large settlement of sixty acres, bounded by a red sandstone wall. Seven tesselated and mosaic pavements were still in position in 1924[22] and five by 1959[23]. These remains reflect a high degree of Romanisation of this northern-most of Roman civil settlements.

Aldborough was inhabited until c390 A.D., York until 428 A.D., and Roman forces finally left Britain in the same year. There is still much to be unearthed, literally, about this late stage of the Roman occupation and about what replaced it, but the archaeological evidence from Ilkley fort is that there was no sudden destruction of the buildings or early post Roman occupations.[24] Do we visualise the ruins of the stone buildings

and walls of the Romans standing there much as those of a dissolved priory stand today, until just before the Conquest, when faced stone was robbed for the building of the church and much later that of the manor house? At some time a religious site must have developed on which the Anglo-Saxon crosses were erected. Was there any continuity between a later Roman, Christian site and an early Anglian Christian one?

To what extent has the Roman network of forts and roads influenced the later layout of the patterns of communication and settlement? The Roman forts and settlements shown on fig. 7 and lying within the Dales all still have settlements on or near them. The forts, echoing the road pattern, lie on the Wharfe–Aire gap axis, the west edge of the Plain of York and the Stainmore gap, which links the Eden and Tees valleys. Only Bainbridge and Reeth lay well within the Dales, the remainder were very much fringe forts to the Dales area proper. Because of their strategic importance, the Roman fort sites were bound to be used by later peoples, but the evidence is that they were left derelict for a considerable period of time after the Romans departed in the early fifth century. The existence of building materials may have attracted later peoples back to their sites. The roads too, seem to have suffered a similar fate: sections can be picked out and short stretches have been used as part of present day roads, but new highways have followed the broad lines of the roads rather than the exact line. The Roman road from Burrow-in-Lonsdale to Bainbridge for example, is used by the Ingleton–Hawes road as far as Ribblehead but from there it has ceased to be the line of a modern road. The present roads link valley heads together; the strategic significance of Burrow-in-Lonsdale and Bainbridge has been replaced by the market functions of Ingleton and Hawes. The medieval and modern roads avoided the exposed heights of Carr Fell at Drumaldrace, yet the Romans cut their road right across some very difficult country: interestingly the Pennine Way follows the line of the Roman road from Carr End north-west to the foot of Dodd Fell. The physical geography of the Dales was more serious a check to medieval travellers and traders than to the Roman military units who carried their defences with them and constructed their temporary staging camps en route.

The Saxon and Scandinavian phase 400 A.D.—1066 A.D.

After the departure of the Romans in the early part of the fifth century A.D. the period often termed the Dark Ages began. The Dark Ages are less dark to those interested in the story of the development of our

21. The Roman fort at Bainbridge (Cambridge University Collection). 22. Foundations of town wall and exposed interval tower at Aldborough (James Guilliam).

countryside than they were 100 years ago. The gradual examination of Saxon and Danish charters, the study of the origins of place names, the work of an increasing number of professionally trained archaeologists and of architectural historians is all combining to provide us with a rather more detailed picture of the period within which many of our existing settlements originated.

The study of the evolution of the place names of Yorkshire has culminated in the important eight volume work on the *Place Names of the West Riding* by J. H. Smith.[25] He has shown that many of the settlement names in the Dales are either Saxon or Scandinavian in origin. The pre-Roman Celtic peoples had named many natural features and those of a number of the rivers and of the major hills have survived in their Celtic form: names such as those of the Dee, Swale and Ure and those of Pen-y-ghent and Addleborough all show Celtic origins. The burgh element reflects the existence of sites that were once fortified as in Ingleborough (Celtic) and Aldborough (Roman). The danger of placing too much emphasis of place name derivations however, is perhaps emphasised by the fact that Elslack, Bainbridge and Ilkley forts have not been left with 'burgh' or even 'caister' place elements as claims to their archaeologically proven Roman origins, though Dodsworth did write of Burwens Camp at Elslack.

A. H. Smith points out that Ripon is a name of 'great antiquity' and links it with Ripley and a lost Ripestic. As the area between Nidd and Ure was referred to as Riponshire in medieval times, he suggests that it may represent an early area of Anglian settlement by the Hrypa folk. Repton in Nottinghamshire may be from the same derivation. He suggests that Markingfield and Markington, south of Ripon, may imply settlements on the boundary of the Hrypa area. He sees the Ham and Ingaham (pre-Viking) place names as showing evidence of early Saxon settlement in Wharfedale, Airedale and Nidderdale with another area of early settlement around Clapham and Bentham. The 'tons' reflect a spread of Saxon settlement north and west. He also draws attention to the significance of the 800ft. contour as marking the height limit of the Saxon, pre-Viking settlement.

The influence of Saxon settlement is seen especially in the –ham, –ton, –ing and –ley place name endings. It is interesting that Wensleydale shows the former two elements strongly whereas Wharfedale has many places with the –ley suffix. Mid-Wensleydale has Castle Bol*ton*, Pres*ton*, Wit*ton* and Bur*ton* all very near together: in Wharfedale Leath*ley*, O*tley*, Bur*ley* and Ilk*ley* all may imply the former existence of woodland as –ley is derived from O.E., leah—a clearing. However, as Smith points out, it can denote glade or even open land, so that specific woodland clearance should not always be assumed as being implied by this element. Certain patterns appear in the names of certain areas: naming can be seen from the map to be a non-random process and therefore it can be concluded to have significance in its patterns.

Sudden interesting changes in name types appear so that in Wensleydale a few miles west of the –tons we find Buttersett, Appersett and Countersett, all occurring near Semerwater on the south side of the main valley. The suffix –sett in upland areas is usually interpreted as being derived from the Norse saeter implying a temporary summer settlement. Many other names of the dales are largely Scandinavian in origin. Scandinavian is stated advisedly because Danish invaders came in the tenth century from the east and Norsemen came down the Irish Sea from the Hebrides or even from Ireland and moved up the Ribble and Lune valleys in Lancashire and then over into the heads of the eastwards running valleys.

The 10 square kilometre sample area around Hellifield, shows the names of the main settlements within it and the meanings of the names as given by Smith. This area is part of the area that Smith suggests experienced a much stronger Anglo/Saxon influence than that of the hills to the north. It is an area in the main of Saxon tuns or farmsteads. Nearly all the names, excepting Agden (a topographical description), already existed by the time of the Domesday Survey in 1086. Even Newsholme and Newton were 'new' before 1086. The secondary names shown on the one-inch map in the sample area are in the main descriptive. In Swinden parish, for example, Swinden Gill Wood and Swinden Moor Head are marked as is Cobers Laithe, a barn named after a family. Paythorne in Gisburn Forest has the Thorners (West, North and Lower), the Agdens and Tewitt Hall to the north west: these all suggest woodland in the main and Tewitt Hall implies the haunt of the peewit. The small, glacial hills of the Craven lowlands are usually termed –ber: from beorg (A/S–hill) or berg (Norse–hill).

Smith argues that in West Staincliff (the Wapentake in which the area shown lies) 37% of the main names have Scandinavian origins whereas in Ewcross (see map) 65% show a Scandinavian influence. He suggests that the Malham area underwent primary colonisation by Norse settlers.

By the eleventh century the Celtic, Saxon and Scandinavian elements were cohering within the physical units of the dales. The Danes had devastated York in their raids of the ninth and tenth centuries but later they became settlers. The Scots (Picts) were raiding the region in all probability before the Norman Conquest (see next chapter). Settlements that had been established during the Saxon period were in some cases destroyed by the early Scottish raids but many others were to suffer more severely still when the Normans devastated much of the area after the Conquest.

Place name elements in the Dales
(of main places)

A. Anglo/Saxon

1. *Early*	ham	e.g. Clapham
	ingham	e.g. Addingham
	Settlement usually with a group or personal name.	
2. *Later*	ton (farm)	e.g. Horton
	ley (clearing)	e.g. Otley
3. *Mercian*	worth (enclosure)	e.g. Wigglesworth
	scip (sheep)	e.g. Skipton
4. *Northumbrian*	scep (sheep)	e.g. Sheepscar
5. *Descriptive names*	e.g. dene = valley ; ber = hill ; etc.	

B. Scandinavian

1. *Norse*	by (farmstead)	e.g. Kirkby
	skali	Shieling—summer hut e.g. Scales
	toft	curtilage
	garth	enclosure
	bekki	stream
	gil	ravine
	brattr	short
	brekka	slope
	slakki	hollow
	eng	meadow
	haugr	hill
	kelde	spring
	kjarr	marsh
2. *Danish*		
	thorp	secondary settlement
	both	booth
	brink	slope
	hulin	water meadow
	klint	rock

C. Post Conquest
Names implying sub-division e.g. high, low ; east, west ; new.
Names with monastic links, e.g. Abbey, Abbots, Monks, Grange.
Names with links by family, office or activity e.g. Burton *Constable* (office)
Newton *Banks* (family)
Kirkby *Overblow* (iron making)

D. Minor place names e.g. Distinctive places within a parish were often named descriptively after locally occurring trees, other vegetation, state of ground, etc.

Place elements in a sample area of 10 kms square in the mid Ribble Valley as shown on Fig. 8.
AS = Anglo-Saxon   N = Norse
1. Martins Both (mere :tun) = farm near a pool.
2. Ingthorpe(unkel :thorpe) N = Personal name ; outlying farmstead (presumably with reference to Martin).
3. Stainton (stan :tun) = stony + farmstead.
4. Coniston (konungr's :tun) (AS) = King's farmstead.
5. Otterburn (oter :burn) (AS) = the other stream.
6. Airton (Aire :tun) (AS) = farmstead on the Aire.
7. Scosthrop (Scott :thorpe) (N) = Scott (Irish Vikings) outlying farmstead.

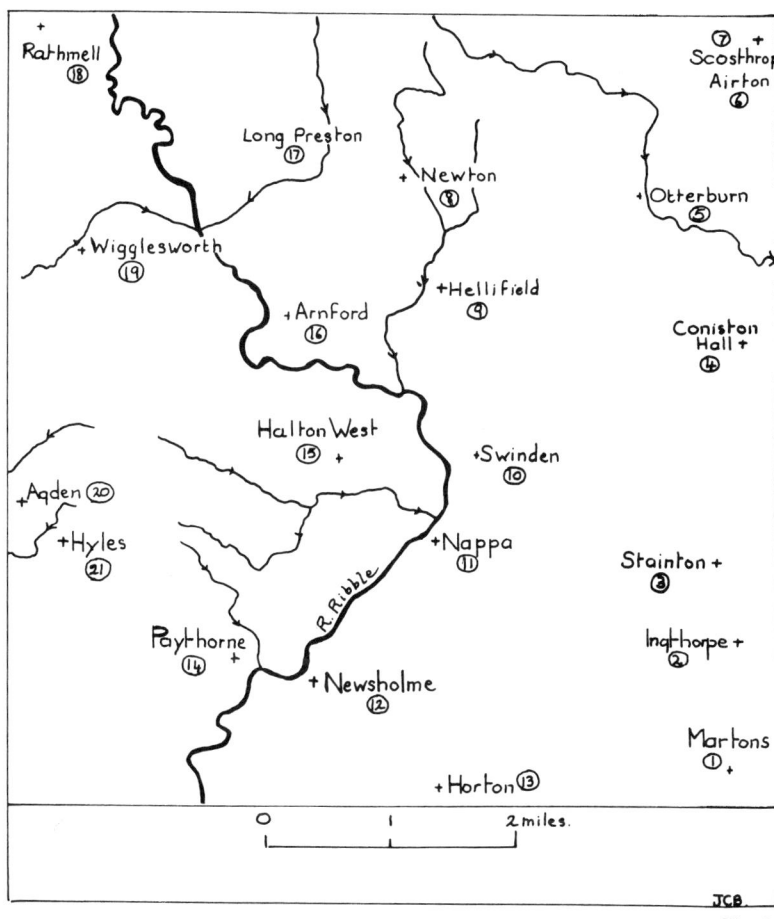

Fig. 8.

8. Newton (New:tun) = the new farmstead.
9. Hellifield (Helgi:field) (N) = Helgi's open land.
10. Swinden (swin:denn) (AS) = swine valley.
11. Nappa (knaepp) = bowl (either hollow or in verted).
12. Newsholme (AS) = new houses.
13. Horton (horu:tun) (AS) = farm on dirty land.
14. Paythorne (pai:thorn) (N) = pai (personal name, the peacock) and thorn. Pie as in magpie might be more likely.
15. Halton (halh:tun) (AS) = farmstead in the nook, hollow, corner of land or water meadow.
16. Arnford (aerne:ford) (AS) = ford which can be crossed by riding.
17. Preston (priest's:tun) (AS) = priest's farmstead.
18. Rathmell (ranthr:melr) (AS) = red sand-bank.
19. Wigglesworth (wincels:worth) (AS) = Wincel's enclosure.
20. Agden (ac:dene) (AS) = Oak valley.
21. Hyles (hygel) = hillock.

General Texts
Elgee, F. & H., *The Archaeology of Yorkshire*, London 1933.
Victoria County History of Yorkshire, Vol. II.
Beresford, M. W., & Jones, G. R. J., *Leeds and its Region*, Leeds 1967, VIIa, VIIb, VIIc, VIII.
Edwards, W., *An Early History of the North Riding*, London 1924.
Hartley, B. R., 'Some problems of the Roman Military Occupation of the North of England', *Northern History*, I, 1966/7, 7–20.

References
[1] E. T. Cowling, *Rombalds Way: a prehistory of Mid-Wharfedale*, Otley 1946, II, 7–30.
[2] A. Raistrick, 'The Bronze Age in West Yorkshire', *Y.A.J.*, XXIX, 1929.
[3] N. Thomas. The Thornborough Circles, near Ripon. *Y.A.J.* XXXVIII.
[4] Cowling, V, 76–105. Useful bibliography given.
[5] Cowling, VI, 118.
[6] Cowling, V, 94.
[7] R. Pedley, 'The Brigantes in Britain.' *Trans. Architectural and Archaeological Society of Durham and Northumberland*, VIII, 1937, 24–42.
[8] R. Pedley, 38.
[9] M. Wheeler, 'The Stanwick Fortifications.' *Society of Antiquaries Research Report*, XVII, 1954.
[10] M. Wheeler.
[11] A. King, *Early Pennine Settlement*, Clapham 1970, 67–70.
[12] Cowling, VIII, 129–152.
[13] A. Raistrick.
[14] A. Raistrick, *Malham and Malham Moor*, Clapham 1947.
[15] Cowling, IX, XX.
[16] King, 67–70.
[17] Wheeler.
[18] B. R. Hartley, 'The Roman Fort at Ilkley.' *Proc. of the Leeds Philosophical and Literary Society*, XII, 1966, 23–72.
[19] B. R. Hartley, 'The Roman Fort at Bainbridge: Excavations 1957–9.' *Proc. of the Leeds Philosophical Society*, IX, 1960, 107–31.
[20] I. D. Margary, *Roman Roads in Britain*, Vol. II, London 1957, Fig. 3, III & IV.
[21] Elgee, 135.
[22] Edwards, 17.
[23] N. Pevsner, *Yorkshire West Riding*, Penguin, 1967, 77.
[24] Hartley, 19, above.
[25] J. H. Smith, *The Place Names of the West Riding of Yorkshire*, Vols. I–VIII (1961–3).

3
The Story of Settlement
Norman times to the late 17th Century

The Norman Settlement

The record of what the Normans found twenty years after the Conquest is in the Domesday Book. Professor H. C. Darby and I. S. Maxwell have discussed the implications of this record in their *Domesday Geography of Northern England*.[1] The wasting of the North and West Ridings is the outstanding feature to which they draw attention.[2] Hellifield for example, was recorded as being laid waste; two separate mentions for it in folio 332 of Domesday Book record neither population or value for 1066–1086. The lack of a value in 1066 suggests that Scottish raiding had perhaps already laid the vill waste. Otley together with its berewicks in 1086 is recorded as having its greater part as waste but for 1066 5 sokemen, 11 villeins, 19 bordars and 1 priest were given as its population and its value fell from £10 in 1066 to £3 in 1086, a big fall in 20 years.

It seems likely that the picture was even more complicated than was first realised. It may be that new Norman landowners on the Vale of York whose lands were devastated, perhaps by Scots and Danes between 1069 and 1076 or by the Norman Conquest of 1069–1070, then replenished their lands with population from their less prosperous Pennine vills so that the uplands were depopulated but not waste. Bishop has suggested this as an explanation for the observation that Ilbert de Laci held lands divided between the Pennines and the Wharfe–Aire basin and that 907 of the people of his lands were in the latter areas whereas his upland vills were 'almost entirely abandoned'.[3] A similar situation was true of the lands of Count Alan in the North Riding in his Honour of Richmond.

Whatever the detailed explanations may be, the result was one of an almost complete depopulation throughout the whole of Craven and Upper Wharfedale. It was a vacuum into which later Norman and post Norman settlement, following in the main from monastic land grants, could flow. However, not all areas were heavily devastated and one that escaped relatively lightly seems to have been that to the west of Richmond, within the triangle bounded by Richmond, Leyburn and Masham. Why this area should escape is not entirely clear.

The domesday map is, unfortunately, one that can only be partly reconstructed; it is known that only a small proportion of the churches that actually existed were recorded and also that not all the mills were detailed. Woodland was mentioned in the Yorkshire folios by size instead of by the number of swine it could feed as was done in East Anglia. Kirkby Malzeard's entry for example, noted the existence of an underwood one league long and one broad (a league is normally interpreted in the Domesday Book as 12 furlongs or 1½ miles). The West Riding woodlands mapped by Darby and Maxwell show no entry in the Dales proper and a gap between Boroughbridge and Knaresborough.[4] All in all the information given for woodlands is odd: it seems unlikely that woodland did not exist in so many parts of the Dales as early as 1086 and indeed if areas remained free of people and more especially of their stock, woodland would begin to re-establish itself quite fast.

Although many settlements can be shown on place name evidence to be pre-Conquest it does seem that the Norman invasion must have led to a

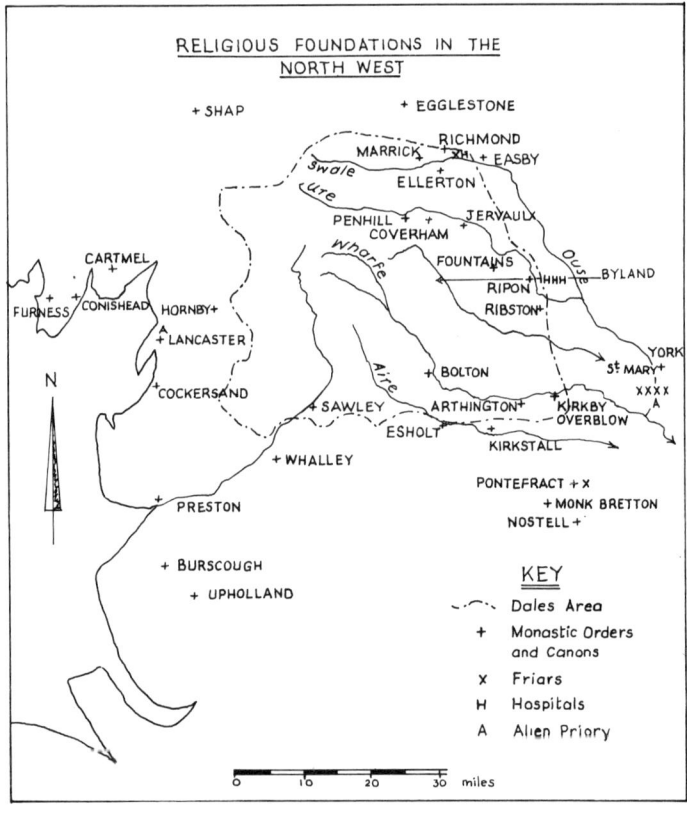

Fig. 9.

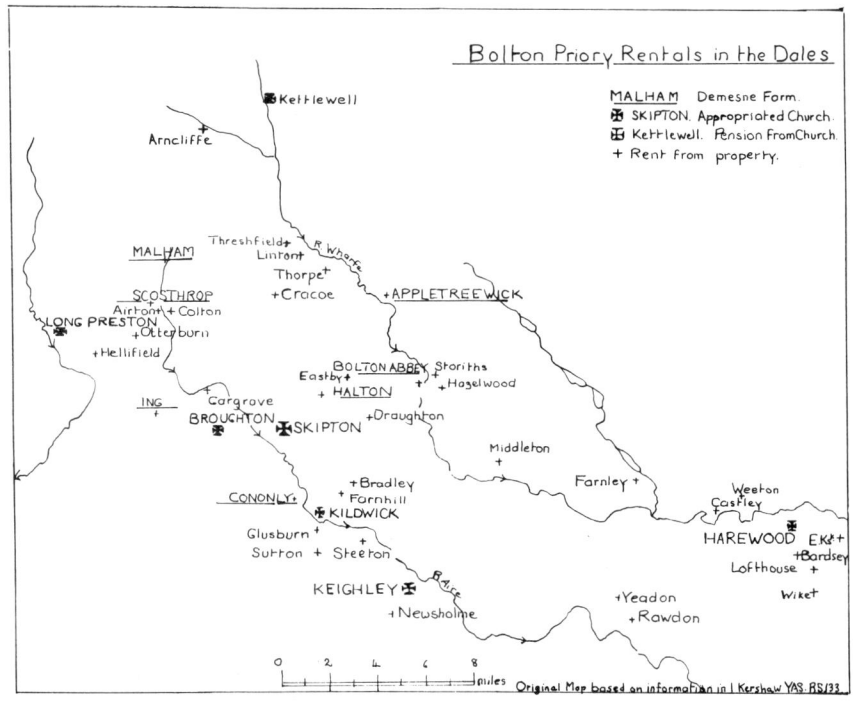

Fig. 10.

temporary break in their continuity. It was the work of the new owners, frequently abbeys, to begin to re-settle old sites, perhaps on a new plan and to extend colonisation further into the Dales proper. The many new monastic houses were very important in beginning this work wherever they were granted lands.

Abbeys

As figs. 9 and 10 show, the various monastic houses within the Dales had interests which, whilst they were concentrated near to the abbey precincts, also spread far. Other abbeys, such as Furness in the southern Lake District and Kirkstall, had much land within the Dales. It is difficult to make any accurate statistical assessment of the proportion of land that was to some degree tied to a monastic house for payment either of rents (because they were Lords of the Manor) or tithes (because the local church had been 'given' to the abbey) but in much of the Dales it must have been perhaps, 25 per cent of the total.

What we can see on the ground from this period that begins with the

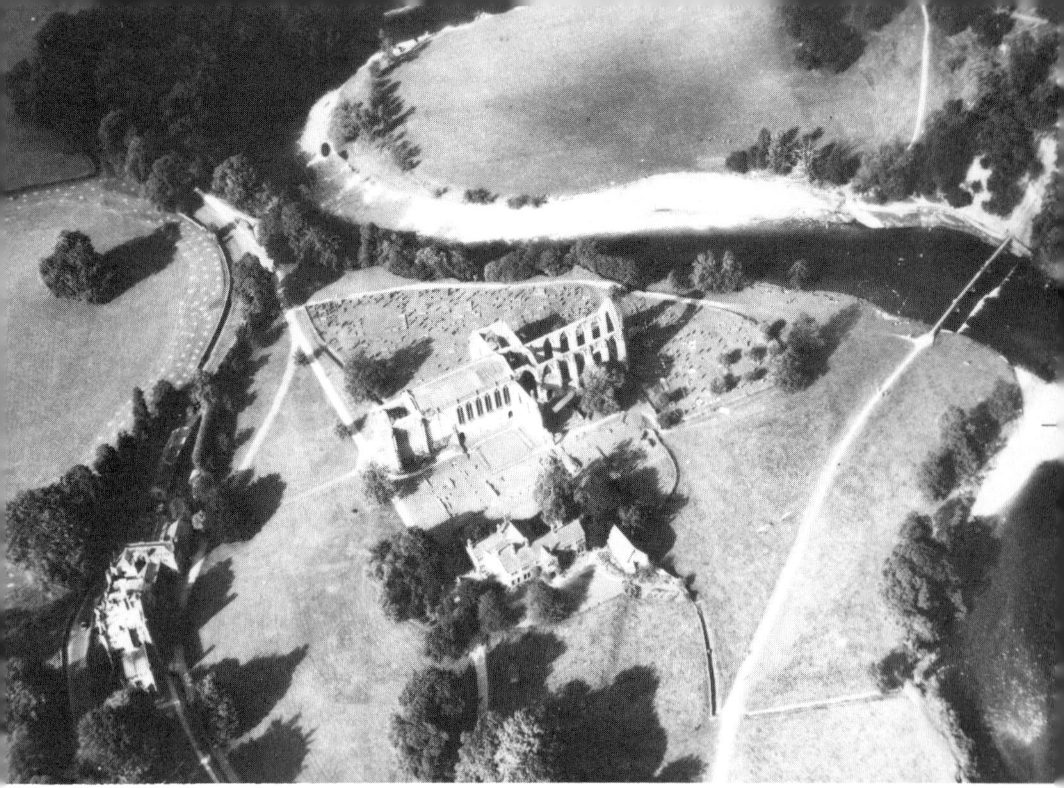

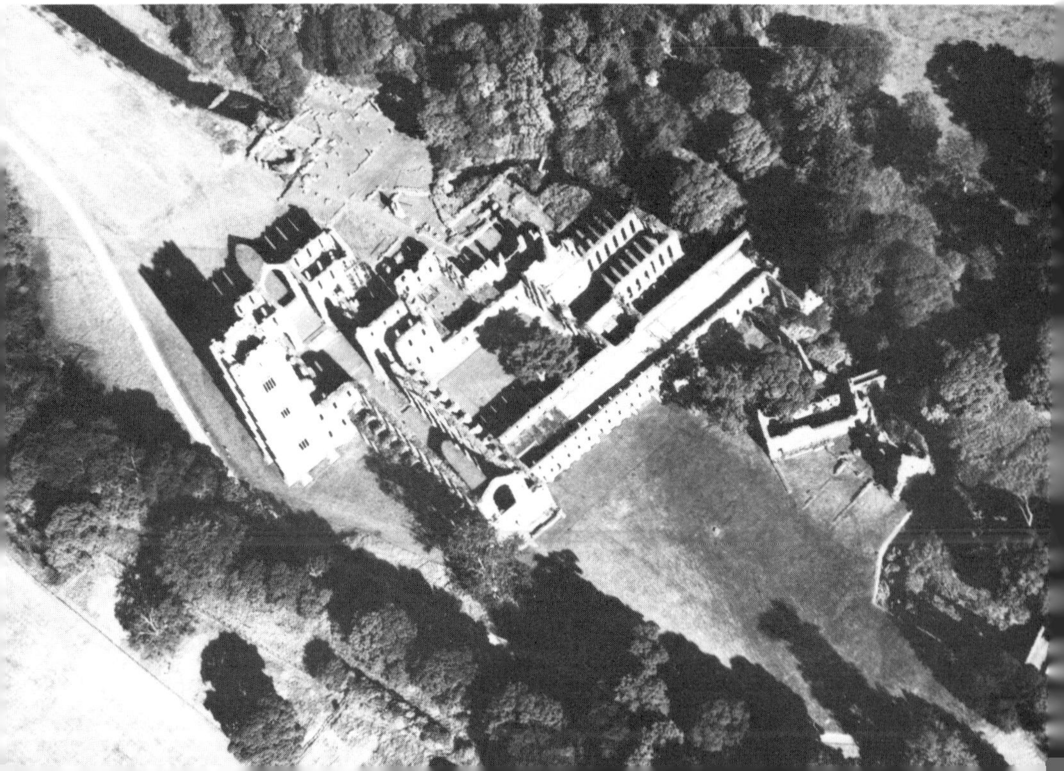

foundation of Sawley (photo 27) and ends with the Dissolution (c1535) is a number of fine ruins and of former monastic granges and/or manor houses that have survived to become very important focal points within the Dales or near to them (photos 23–29). Bolton Abbey and Fountains Abbey are perhaps the two best known examples. The names of whole areas of fell still bear the mark of the monastic period, for example Abbotside near Wensley (fig. 11). This area formerly belonged first to Fors Abbey and later after its refounding, to Jervaulx Abbey. The hunting parks of the abbots and their lodges have in many cases survived as modern estates. The precincts of Fountains and Bolton have survived to this day: Kirkstall (just outside our area) has had a very different history but even there, the great spread of the Cistercian ruins has survived the encroachment of Leeds.

The monastic houses had not only importance because of the sites of their ecclesiastical and domestic buildings. They were also a very important group of new landowners in the Dales. It must be remembered that some great gifts of land to the church had been made well before the Normans arrived: the Liberty of Ripon, for example, was derived from grants of land made to the Archbishop of York as was that of the Manor of Otley. The evolution of the monastic systems built on the models of the mother houses of Cîteaux and Sées and Premonstré in Normandy, and the pattern of the religious beliefs of people in the 11th and 12th centuries meant that many great landowners made gifts of lands, or of the income from parish churches on their lands, to a particular monastic order in return for services to be held in their memory and for certainty of places of burial. Thus we see the foundation and building of great monastic houses. Once built, other benefactors gave them more land and so gradually they became considerable landowners throughout the region (fig. 10). As has been said earlier, when much of the land was waste these religious houses could provide important focal points for the re-settlement of the region. Their abbots and priors became very influential people in the area and their economic activities created new patterns of settlement and movement within the region.

Perhaps the most dramatic illustration of the scale of the influence of these houses is to be seen in the naming of a western Pennine fell as Fountains Fell. This area, a high block of moorland together with the richer limestone pastures on its lower slopes, was in effect a sheep and cattle ranch for the monks of Fountains Abbey. Their droveways to it and granges along the route survive. For example, the monks of Fountains, or their lay brothers,

23. Bolton Priory.   **24.** Fountains Abbey. (Cambridge University Collection).

Monastic ruins (opposite page). **25, 26** (top). Fountains Abbey – tower and 13th century detail; the Norman south aisle. **27.** Sawley Abbey.
Fountains Abbey farmsteads (this page). **28.** Nether Bordley: Bordley Hall. **29.** Lainger House, Bordley.

had an important grange (out farm) at Kilnsey and from Kilnsey their track to Fountains Fell has survived as Mastiles Lane. A section of the rental of 1456/7 even gives some idea of a rent collector's route as the farms, all still surviving with little changed names, were listed[5]:

	£	s	d	
de Mallom (Malham)	13	2	8	Malham
de molend ibidem (the mill there)	2	0	0	
de Scothorpe (Scosthrop)	0	9	0	Airedale
de Calton (Calton)	1	0	0	
de Preston (Long Preston)	0	19	0	
de Arnsford (Arnforth)	8	0	0	Ribblesdale
de Wygilsworth (Wigglesworth)	1	0	8	Craven
de Holmknotts (?)	2	0	0	Lowlands
de Rughclose (?Rough Close: Fountains Fell)	1	0	0	
de fornagilhows (Fornah Gill: Fountains Fell)	2	0	0	
de Wests hows (?Westside House: Fountains Fell)	2	6	8	Fountains
de Caupanhow (Capon Hall, 2 miles W of Malham Tarn)	2	0	0	Fell &
de Tranhous (Higher and Lower Trenhouse, ½ mile)	1	7	0	Malham
de Tranhoushull (south of Malham Tarn)	2	12	4	
de Mallwater Hous (Malham Tarn House)	1	13	3	
de Mydlehoos (MiddleHouse, 1 mile N.E. Malham Tarn)	1	0	0	
de Colgyhous (Cow Gill House—Bordley)	1	3	4	
de Nederbordley (Bordley Hall?)	6	13	4	
de Langehous (Lainger—Bordley)	4	0	0	
de Neuhous (New House—Bordley)	3	0	0	Bordley
de Colgylcote (Cow Gill Cote—Bordley)	2	6	8	
de Over bordley at folcote (Bordley)	6	13	4	
de Treschfeld (Threshfield)	2	5	10	
de Lynton (Linton)	0	10	4	
de Thorpe (Thorpe-by-Burnsall)	0	4	4	Wharfedale
de Byrnsall (Burnsall)	0	1	0	
de Apiltrwyke (Appletreewick)	0	2	0	
de Hebden (Hebden)	0	8	0	
	71	0	2	

This is the Craven entry in the rental: it forms less than one-tenth of the total Fountains rental for 1456/7 which was over £800. Fountains Abbey had estates even more far flung than this and had legal disputes with its sister Cistercian house of Furness Abbey about rights of grazing in Borrowdale in the Lake District.

Some idea of the nature of life in the Dales during this monastic phase comes from the records of disputes that have survived and that relate to abbey lands. A tithe dispute arose in 1598 between Edward Talbot, farmer of the Rectory of Kirkby Malloughdale, and Thomas Proctor, the occupier of the land at Fornagill on Fountains Fell. In his defence and to support his case that his land should not pay tithe, Proctor called elderly inhabitants to show that the land had been farmed by Fountains stock and should therefore after the dissolution, be free of tithe. One Ralph

Buck, aged 80, of Darnbrook in the Parish of Kirkby Malham said he knew Fornagill for 8 years before the Dissolution and has seen the cattle, horses, etc., brought from Fountains Abbey and 'hath seen the heardes (men) milk the Abbeis Kyne in the same ground lying their swords and bucklers besides them whilst they were milking'! Whatever the solution to the dispute may have been this picture of life on pre-dissolution Fountains Fell is a nice one: it is interesting to note that cattle and horses seem to be more important than sheep in this description.[6]

At Bolton Priory the rental taken in 1539 at the Dissolution mentions an interesting variety of stock and crops held in the buildings of the Priory:-

(a) 22 shillings for 30 bushels of various kinds of grain found in the granary.
(b) £10 for 40 acres of arable land sown with wheat and rye, thus sold to the said Thomas Proctor upon the dissolution at 5s 0d per acre.
(c) £18 for the price of 20 quarters of wheat and 100 quarters of oats found in sheaves stored within the barns of the late monastery there; sold to Thomas Proctor.
(d) £62.17.8 for the price of cattle found there and sold to the same Thomas Proctor

—33 oxen price	£15.6.8
—9 stotts with 1 bull	£4.10.0
—9 cows with 3 bulls	£27.2.0
—8 young beasts	£0.4.0
—20 oxen which were lent	£13.19.0;

and of £18.15.0 for the price of 102 ewes at 14 pence apiece: that is 119 shillings

—80 wethers at 14 pence apiece that is £4.13.4
—122 wethers found at Newhouse at 16d apiece, £8.2.8 sold to Thomas Proctor;

and of 36 shillings for the price of 4 stotts found in the custody of the wife of (?) Stanley, from loan by the late Abbott sold to Thomas Proctor and of £4.0.0 for the price of 16 horses and foals . . . sold wholesale to Thomas Proctor . . .[7]

The Dissolution Rental goes on to describe various farms for which the Priory received rents. In Storiths with Hazlewood:-

'£6.18.3 for the farm of our tenement with appurtances called the Stedehouse (Park House Farm) with tithes of grain falling within the said tenement and with le browsyng from trees called Holles, thus demised to Alice, widow late the wife of John Pettye . . . for a term of 41 years rendering yearly therefrom 24 calves £4.00, 50 stone of cheese 29/5, 25 stone of butter 18/9, for le browsying 3/4 and for the Said tithes, 7/- . . . to be paid yearly in equal portions . . . now in the tenure of . . . Henry Earl of Cumberland.'

The complexities of the accounting need not concern us but the nature of the farming is interesting in both these examples. The former is perhaps the more interesting in that wheat and rye were being grown in the neighbourhood of the priory—an area where cereal crops are rarely grown now. The Storiths example, despite the mention of tithes payable on grain, appears to have its income in the main from its stock and their products: again as on Fountains Fell cattle play a more important part in these accounts than do sheep.

Lay Lords

The impact of the Normans on land tenure by means of grants to lay lords and to monasteries and churches, is dealt with specifically in the next chapter. This section is more concerned with the impact the Norman Conquest had on the development of settlement. The population recovered from the devastation by William I and it is now accepted that England's population reached a peak in the early fourteenth century before climatic deterioration and the Black Death caused severe reduction in numbers.

Much of the Dales was royal hunting forest until the seventeenth century and it may have been leased out to wealthy lords from time to time. The pre-eminence of the deer discouraged the rapid growth of settlement but lodges, warreners' houses, enclosing walls, fences and access roads were all necessary. A Craven charter noted that Alice de Rumilly granted 'every tenth beast taken in her demesne woods and chases in Craven' to the Canons of Embsay (who later moved to Bolton) in 1155/6 A.D.[8]

In 1307 horses ousted deer in the park of Skipton Castle: an inquisition found that the former keeper of the castle, one Richard Oyset, had overstocked the park with seventy mares 'so that the deer were put to flight, only eleven does and a buck remaining because the park was small and only a league in circumference'. The same inquisition also noted timber clearance—'a large number of oaks in various woods had been sold to iron forges and divers persons'.

Some settlements have changed significantly so that what may now survive as a farmhouse or hamlet may once have been separately recorded. The major area in the Dales for which a number of sites has been recorded is that of Claro wapentake (fig. 11). Azerley, a mile east of Kirkby Malzeard, had 122 taxpayers in 1377 yet it has since been absorbed into a park and has disappeared. Clotherholme lay two miles west north-west of Ripon on the north bank of the River Laver. It was a taxed settlement in 1297 but by 1811 it was reduced to eight families (perhaps 50 people); it struggled on with a population of 10 in 1841 but has since become a suburb of Ripon. Givendale, two miles south-east of Ripon, had a watermill in 1250 and eight taxpayers in 1297: it too has become a Ripon suburb in recent years. In Nidderdale, Eaveston, four miles north-west of Pateley Bridge, was separately assessed in 1297: as late as 1520 evictions from it were reported to the Star Chamber.[10]

Major factors quoted for change are usually those of disease and of enclosing or encroachment by landowners. The example given as a sample of eleven listed by Beresford in Claro show that a wider range of factors is at work in influencing the relative growth or decline of settlements: the growth or collapse of rural industry and of particular family fortunes such as the Scropes of Bolton, may provide localised factors that do not run along the national patterns. Stenningford, one and a half miles south-east of West Tanfield, illustrates this: it was burnt by the Scots and later probably finished off by enclosure for grazing grounds. By the early 1950s

30. Bolton Castle, Wensleydale, c 1378. The Scrope family stronghold.

far more sites had been found by Beresford in Claro than in Skyrack or Staincliffe wapentakes: none were listed for Ewcross and the difference between wapentakes is not easily explained.

The very fact that much land in the Dales was given by big landowners to monastic houses has meant that major archives such as those of the Lords of Skipton or those of institutions such as abbeys, give a valuable record not only of the gifts but also reveal something of the nature of the properties being donated or received. More often they tell of pieces of land and of its character, sometimes they may tell of buildings, of mills or of roadways and also of the extent to which land is wooded.

The existence of some sort of field system can be deduced from gifts such as that in 1180–1200 by Harsqui de Hetton and Ingeleive his wife to Furness Abbey of two acres of land in the field of Hetton in Hungerhill, lying in length by a ditch dividing the fields of Hetton and Winterburn.[11] Another example was that in 1219 of 'a gift by William de Marton to Bolton Priory of a culture of land [implying arable land] in the territory of Marton called Ingthorpe . . . with common pasture'.[12] Finally, in 1175–1190 Walter de Fauconberg made a gift to Fountains Abbey of six bovates of land in the field of Kettlewell.[13] (A bovate was between 5 and 32 acres in Yorkshire).[14] The implications of these twelfth and thirteenth century charters are that a field system was in operation in these townships but that it was a single field system, perhaps of the infield outfield type rather than anything like the orthodox three field type so frequently quoted as the medieval model of a field system. The use of the term land seems to imply that arable land is being dealt with in these gifts.

The early charters may also reveal much about stock keeping practices too. In 1210–1220, Peter de Meaux gave a bovate of land in Malham to Bolton Priory and a site for making a sheepfold there which Hugh had given him by the sheepfold of William de Malham, sufficient for 300 sheep with common pasture of the vill.[15] Many of the early charters are concerned with such rights, with the definition of grazing boundaries and rather later with the numbers of stock to be allowed on common grazings as population and therefore the numbers of their stock rise. Most cattle rights went with particular properties but sheep rights more often seem to stay with the lord or his tenant (sub-lord) as manorial rights and therefore provided a greater source of conflict between lord and manorial tenants.

The stock rearing emphasis in the Dales economy is illustrated time and again in tenancy agreements. In 1496 a Mashamshire rental recorded that Richard Beckwith of Nutwith (one mile south-east of Masham) held it for a rental of thirty shillings a year and that he was to keep 20 cattle for the abbey and to return the following annually

13 stone 4 lbs of butter at 12d per stone
26 stone 8 lbs of cheese at 8d per stone
10 stirketts at 4/- each.[16]

Richard held this lease for a term of 48 years. The equivalent cash values suggest that he was already able to pay in rent rather than kind if he so wished but it stresses that it was a pastoral basis upon which the economy of the farm was built. As this was an abbey lease it is possible that this was traditionally a dairy 'grange' of the abbey in origin.

Shafts of light are occasionally thrown by sources such as those just quoted on other miscellaneous elements that may have survived to the present day. The Fountains Abbey rental already quoted referred to Malham Tarn House and to Malham Mill in the late fifteenth century. An earlier charter dated early thirteenth century refers to a grant made by William de Marton to Sallay Abbey of a road to Stainton Grange which had been in dispute, the road to be 20 feet wide for the abbey's carts and other necessaries.[17]

In 1233–43 an agreement was made between the prior and canons of Bolton Priory and William Mauleverer of Beamsley concerning the rights of grinding corn at Beamsley Mill. William agreed to give materials 'in the wood called Blarbanch for repairing their mill pools'.[18]

In 1176, Adam, son of Norman, made a gift to Sawley Abbey of five acres of land in the territory of Weston near Otley for the construction of buildings for the abbey grange of Askwith.[19] Whilst such a charter tells us that new buildings were to be built it implies that a grange was already there and the place named Askwith (Ashwood) may be late and descriptive or earlier and that of a settlement taking its name from the cleared ashwood. The implication is not that of a new place in 1176 but of a place already existing when it was given to Sawley.

One early reference to two bridges in the Dales is made in a charter of 1170–1190 in which William Mauleverer granted the foundations of bridges across the Skirfare and Wharfe to Fountains Abbey and a road 30 feet in width between them.[20]

Progress during these centuries was by no means steady. The raids of the Scots or a period of successive poor harvests could soon cause real distress, especially perhaps if the population had increased in a run of good years. In 1428 John Kempe, Archbishop of York, was 'met at Wensley church by the abbots of Jervaulx and Coverham . . . who informed him . . . that the countryside was too greatly impoverished by failure of crops, murrains, etc., to bear the heavy cost' of a visitation.[21]

A very detailed survey of the Manor of Wensley throws light on the scale and manner of life in Wensleydale in the early seventeenth century.[22] The manor was defined as the possessions of the abbey of Jervaulx in the forest of Wensleydale, north of the Ure and was in the hands of the Earl of Lennox. The diagrammatic map (fig. 11) shows the hamlets listed in the survey from Bainbridge to the head of the valley on the north side of the River Ure. The meadows and pastures would be the lower lands and the cattlegates would lie on the upper valleys. The area described as Cote Moor, Little Fell and Meawes was clearly the area marked now on the O.S. map as Cotterdale Common.

The holdings spread between five acres and 100 in the main, but six tenants were farming more than 100 acres. These six occupied half the meadow and pasture of that occupied by 119 tenants so that they were obviously important local figures.

Manor of Wensley — a survey of holdings, 1614

Acreage	Number	Total acreage
More than 100	6	2054
50–99	14	943
40–49	9	401
30–39	9	300
20–29	13	330
15–19	6	105
10–14	19	235
5–9	21	152
1–4	7	20
less than 1	15	
	119	4543

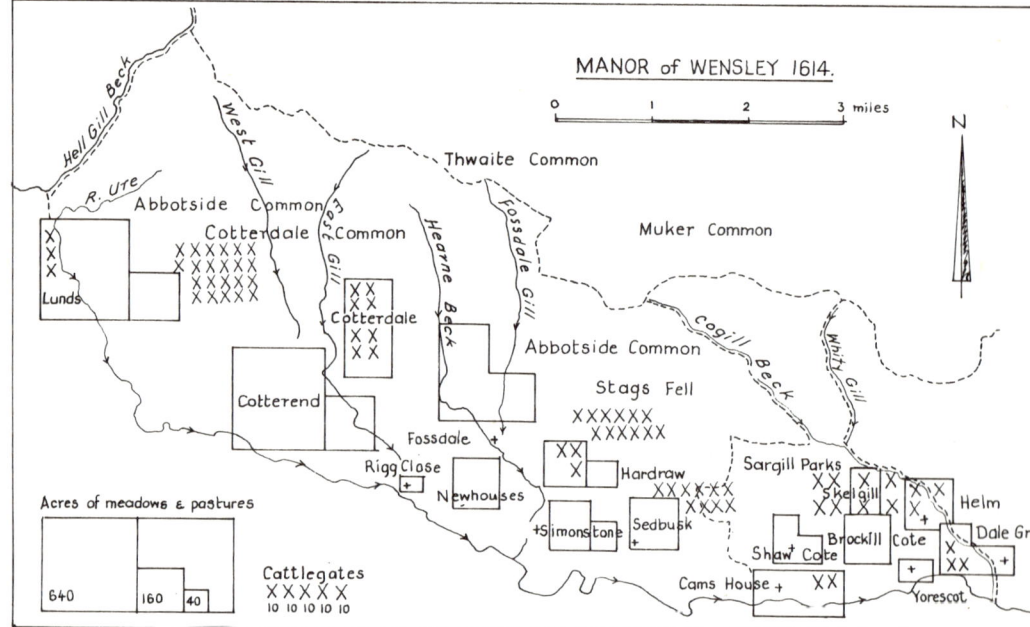

Fig. 11.

Gaudian Bywell of Skellgill is an example of a 'small' tenant farmer. As well as his dwelling house and adjacent garden he rented four parcels of ground totalling sixteen acres. He also had 'belonging to the said tenant' six cattlegates on Coate Moor and two thirds of a cattlegate on Little Fell Meawes. His yearly rent was eleven shillings and one penny. At Yorescot, George Metcalfe lived in more prosperous circumstances. He had 'a mansion house: a barne and a turfehouse called Yorescot with a yarde, a garden and a forstall adjoining and 10 parcels of land lyeing together by the river Yore'. The pieces of land averaged just over four acres each and he had 46 acres. George Metcalfe paid a yearly rent of 46s 8d. There were no cattlegates however with this tenement.

The survey recorded that Coate More (Cote Pasture on the present O.S. map) had 458 acres on which the tenants of Skellgill, Brockellcote, Shawcoates and Jeffrey Prott and Francis Prott of the Hole house had their cattlegates. The same group had a further 64 acres for their cattlegates on Little Fell Meawes on Cotterdale Common as shown on the map.

It seems that holdings such as that of George Metclafe had been either integrated from some earlier system of common meadow management or, more likely because of the forest history of the area, had been created as consolidated holdings during the late colonisation of the upper valley. Assuming that stock provided the main livelihood of the people the need for common 'fields' was much less than in arable areas. Winter feed must however, have been a real problem and hay must have been vital.

An earlier Metcalfe, Thomas, left an inventory in 1577. He lived at Fossdale and was reasonably prosperous leaving £85 of goods and it is interesting to see that almost everything in his farm inventory was livestock—no corn, roots or even hay was listed.

Inventory of Thomas Metclafe of Fossdale, 4 June 1577.

	£	s	d
One stoned horse (gelding)	3	0	0
One mare and one foal	1	13	4
Six old mares	8	0	0
One full stagge (young stallion)	0	13	4
One cold stagge (young gelding)	1	0	0
Three young horse	5	0	0
One old horse	0	10	0
22 tuppes (rams) piggottes (?) and weddetes (castrated male sheep)	3	0	0
73 ewes and gymmers (young ewes)	10	0	0
36 lambs	3	0	0
7 kyne and calves	10	0	0
8 handymylk kyne	9	0	0
2 bulls	2	0	0
3 stottes (year old bull oxen)	3	0	0
12 twynter gwyes (heifer beasts)	8	0	0
4 twynter stottes	3	0	0
10 calves	3	0	0
cheese in the house	0	10	0

23

One hundred years later in 1666/7, yet another of the Metcalfe clan, Richard of Hardraw, left goods worth £62.16.8. He left beef, bacon, cheese and meal worth £1.10.0; hay and corn worth £9.0.0; sixty-seven sheep worth £13.0.0; twenty-two beasts worth £24.10.0 and two horses and a mare worth £6.0.0. Stock formed the bulk of his goods, though hay and corn are mentioned.[24]

At Swinsty in the Washburn valley, Henry Robinson left a very much more lavish inheritance which in 1639 was worth over £700.[25] Cattle of various categories totalled £301.0.0, sheep £85.0.0 and corn and hay £83.0.0. The inventory listed a number of separate barns in which the hay was being kept: wheat, rye and oats were the cereals given. Oxen were used for ploughing and not horses. His farm equipment—two stone wains and three cowpes (lime and dung carts on two wheels or sleds) plus many stone ripping and cutting tools reflected various facets of farm life in the early seventeenth century. The second contribution of sheep to the economy of the period was reflected by Robinson's two pairs of looms, three spinning wheels and thirty stone of wood valued at £18.0.0.

An example from further east, though it is from eighty years earlier, emphasises that the contrasts between the eastern edge of the Dales and that of the higher west held in the sixteenth century just as they do now. Ninian Starsley who lived in Ripon parish and died in 1559, kept fifteen oxen and he grew barley, oats, wheat, red wheat, rye and he had two and a half acres of·peas sown at the time of his death. His cattle, oxen, sheep and horses still dominated the inventory however.[26]

Some late seventeenth century details of agriculture and building pressure come from two Otley rentals of 1692 and 1695. There are frequent mentions of Stakefield, Waterfield and Menshaw Field, but the references are frequently to closes rather than to lands or strips. However, Robert Frankland had '2 acres and an $\frac{1}{2}$ in Stakefield late Caves of Carleton 10d more for one [rood] then late pt of Brearay's oxgang 1d' (oxgangs seemed to be about 7 acres).[27] It seems that inroads on to the commons were being allowed. Richard Norfolk for example, was paying a rent of 4d for 'a cottage and incroachment in Moreside'.[28] This was perhaps a reflection of an increasing population in Otley in the 1690s. The rental gives a number of other examples of the same process.

In the mid-seventeenth century the Civil War caused the decline of some Catholic families and saw the prospering of others. Michael Fawkes of Farnley was fined £360 in November 1646 and in 1652 his estate was sequestered. In fact Farnley survived this trauma, but the Fawkes family suffered relatively to their non-Catholic neighbours.[29] In 1628 the Middleham, Arkengarthdale and New Forest area was sold by King Charles I to the citizens of London, in itself a reflection of a new source of wealth. In 1656 the citizens in turn sold Arkengarthdale to the presumably prospering Dr. J. Bathurst, physician to Oliver Cromwell; he in turn founded a grammar school there in 1659. In short, all sorts of interwoven local and national factors have controlled the way in which settlements change with time. The next chapter considers the organisational frameworks within which communities live and evolve.

References
[1] H. C. Darby and I. S. Maxwell, *Domesday Geography of Northern England*, Cambridge 1962.
[2] as above, figs. 15 and 16.
[3] T. A. M. Bishop, 'The Norman settlement in Yorkshire'. In *Studies in Medieval History*, presented to F. M. Powicke, Oxford 1948, 1–14.
[4] Darby and Maxwell, as above, fig. 12.
[5] J. J. Fowler, editor. 'Memorials of the Abbey of St. Mary of Fountains, Vo. III Bursar's Books, 1456–1459'. *Surtees Society*, 1918, 1, 130, p.11.
[6] *Y.A.S. Record Series*, CXIV, Item 41, p.155.
[7] I. Kershaw, ed., 'Bolton Priory Rentals 1473–1539'. *Y.A.S. Record Series*, CXXXIII, 1969.

[8] Honour of Skipton. E.Y.C., Vol. 7. *Y.R.S. Extra Series*, 5, 1947, Chapter 18.
[9] as above, p.29.
[10] Beresford M., 'The Lost Villages of Yorkshire, Part III West Riding'. *Y.A.J.*, 38, 1952–55, pp215–240.
[11] Honour of Skipton. E.Y.C., Vol. 7. *Y.R.S. Extra Series*, Vol. 5, 1947, Charter 114.
[12] Honour of Skipton, as above, Charter 152.
[13] Honour of Skipton, as above, Charter 141.
[14] I. H. Adams, 'Agrarian Landscape Terms', I.B.G., London, 1976, p.3.
[15] Honour of Skipton, as above, Charter 90.
[16] John Fisher, *The History and Antiquities of Masham and Mashamshire*, London 1815, p.507.
[17] Honour of Skipton, as above, Charter 150.
[18] Honour of Skipton, as above, Charter 77.
[19] Percy Fee. E.Y.C. *Y.R.S. Extra Series*, Vol. IX, 1963, Charter 200.
[20] Honour of Skipton, as above, Charter 86.
[21] A Hamilton Thompson, *The English Clergy of the Fifteenth Century*, 1947.
[22] Yorkshire Surveys. *Y.A.S. Record Series*, CIV, 1941.
[23] H. Thwaite, ed. 'Abstracts of Abbotside Wills, 1552–1638'. *Y.A.S. Record Series*, CXXX, 1967, No. 16.
[24] as above, inV., 4 Feb. 1666/7.
[25] C. D. Brears, 'Yorkshire Probate Inventories'. *Y.A.S. Record Series*, CXXXIV, 1972, p.87.
[26] as above, p.3.
[27] G. E. Kirk, 'Two Rentals of Otley Manor'. *Thoresby Society Publications*, 37, 1945, p.213.
[28] as above, p.211–212.
[29] J. W. Clay, ed., 'Yorkshire Royalist Composition Papers II'. *Y.A.S. Record Series*, XVIII, 1895, No. 167.
[30] *V.C.H. North Riding*, Vol. I, 1914.

4
The Administrative Geography of the Dales
State, Church and the Feudal System

The State
(a) Kingdom

Until the local government reorganisation in April 1974, the Yorkshire Dales lay entirely within one county, although split between two of the three Ridings. Within the Dales local names such as Craven, the Forest of Bowland, Langstrothdale Chase, Uredale and Abbotside are still used. This chapter attempts to unravel names such as these and place them in their geographical and historical contexts. In doing this it is first necessary to look at a larger area than that of the Dales in order to understand the evolution of some of the units.

The earliest unit that seems to have been a forebear of Yorkshire as it existed until 1 April 1974 was the Kingdom of Deira (fig. 12). This was a sixth century early Saxon kingdom which was a component of the larger, better known, Northumbria. Celtic kingdoms such as that of the Brigantes, that of Elmet in the Lower Aire and Calder valleys and perhaps that of Craven may have given early unity to parts of the area that later became Deira. The Saxon earls of the region were the earls of Northumbria, not of Yorkshire. For a short period in early Saxon times Yorkshire, as Deira, had the status of a kingdom: otherwise it was a part of the larger kingdom of Northumbria until the Danish Conquest. The Danes established a kingdom of York, under Halfdan in 875, and this lasted as an independent kingdom until 954 when King Eric Bloodaxe died.[1-2]

(b) County

As a shire, that is an area with its own sheriff and administration responsible to the Crown, Yorkshire was first mentioned in 1065.[3] The peculiarities of the shire boundary are perhaps most marked along its western edge. The river Tees formed a relatively clear cut boundary to the north and the high fells defined the boundary overlooking the Eden Valley but then it crossed the River Rawthey and included half the

Howgill Fells within Yorkshire before following the River Lune and the lower Rawthey. The complexity of the county boundary from the Howgills southwards reflects the involved history of the region; the tenuous links with Richmondshire finally broke and the upstart counties of Cumberland, Westmorland and Lancashire were carved out of an area which was recorded under the main heading of Yorkshire at the time of the making of Domesday Book in 1086. Further south the existence of Cravescire and Norman land grants which led to the consolidation of lands around Lancaster by Roger de Poitou, Skipton by the Percy family and Clitheroe by the Lacys produced the indented county boundary that has only lately been 'rationalised'.

The Dales area, as defined in this book, includes all that area of the North and West Ridings lying within the Pennines that drains in the main to the Yorkshire Ouse. However, problems of definition reflect the long historical wrangles and the complex physical geography further south. Administrative boundaries established by the church, especially that of the ancient Deanery of Craven, itself reflecting an early political unit, were important in making a choice for the south-west corner of the Dales as defined in this study.

So much for the county: what of the Ridings? The first mention of these as units is in 876 A.D.[4] It is suggested that these were a Danish administrative division and that each Riding had its own court as well as being tributary

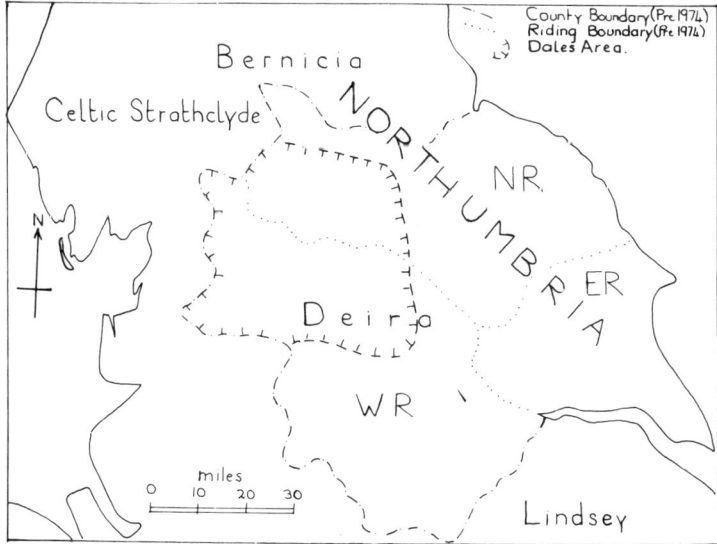

Fig. 12.   Kingdoms, 6th to 9th centuries.

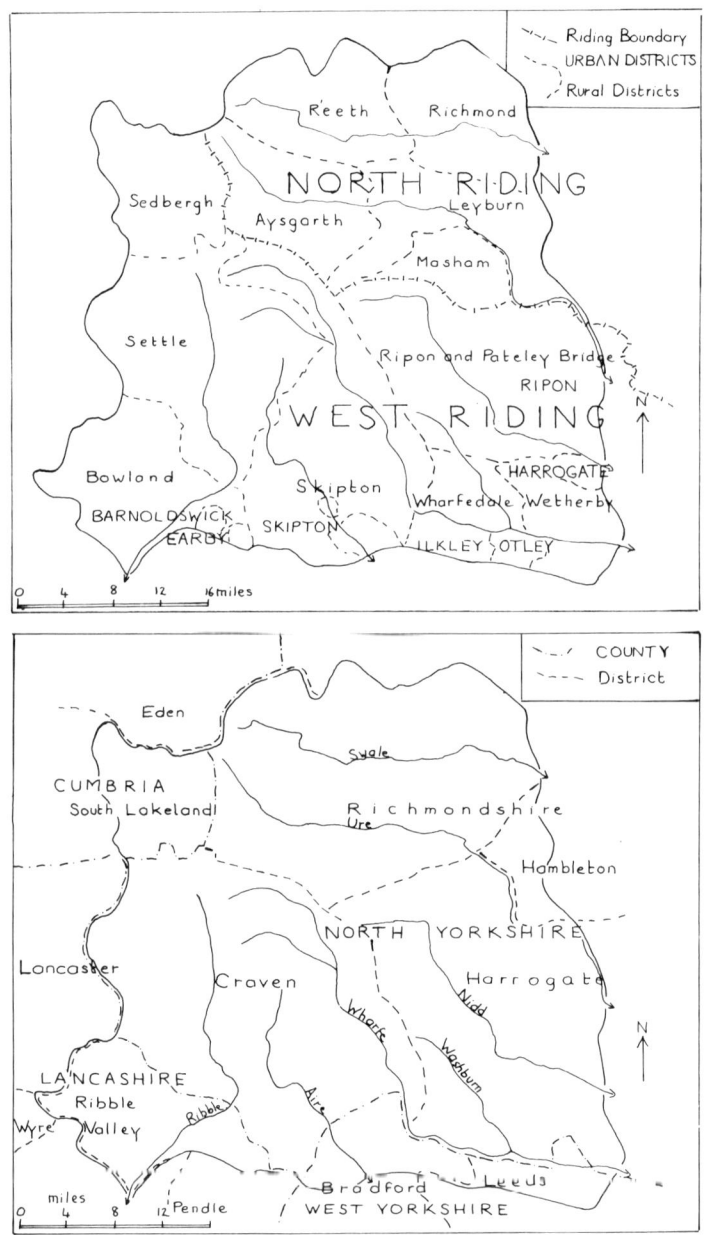

Fig. 13.   Administrative areas in the Dales, pre and post-1974.

to the full shire court of the county. The North Riding court was said to be held under a maple tree near Thirsk; that of the West Riding perhaps at York. As the seat of the archbishop and the site of the County Sheriff's castle and prison, York was the focal point of the whole county from its earliest times. Did the existence of Ridings create secondary centres of importance? It would seem that it did not, at least not until long after the days of Saxon and Danish government. Whilst the three Ridings of Yorkshire became full administrative counties in 1888, their separate existence before then was much more limited. It was not until 1704 that Wakefield was established as the administrative centre for the West Riding; Northallerton had also developed a similar role for the North Riding by the end of the seventeenth century.[6] Baines says of it in 1822, 'the proceedings of the North Riding are a good deal concentrated in the Place,' thereby implying that even then not all administration for the Riding was in fact carried out there.

(c) **Wapentake**

The units of much greater significance than the Ridings were the wapentakes. These were Saxon/Danish units of administration which became significant primarily as the areas which were dealt with by the Crown for the purposes of taxation and for the returns for military service. The first census returns, those for 1801, were collected by wapentakes, and it was only after 1840 that their names gave way to those of the Poor Law Unions. Later the Rural District Councils replaced the Poor Law Unions: even then the Councils often used the boundaries of the ancient wapentakes. The wapentakes of the Dales were mapped after Farrel by Darby and Maxwell on their map of Yorkshire's wapentakes at the time of Domesday Book.[7] As fig. 14 shows, the names given for 1086 are not those which were used later and these have been inserted below. Cravescire and the lands of Count Alan, as shown by Darby and Maxwell, were not technically wapentakes. The wapentakes within those areas are shown by dotted lines: this is particularly important in the case of Richmondshire which was subdivided into several wapentakes. The name Bargescire again implies that a shire was used as the basis for a wapentake.[8] The name Claro was not used until the twelfth century. In view of the marked sub-parallel arrangement of the Dales it is worth noting that the physical layout shows up in the layout of the wapentakes: the Bargescire/Richmond boundary and those between Wharfe and Ure and Wharfe and Nidd do pick out this alignment. Some odd crossings of these wapentake boundaries take place—the parish of Ilkley, for example, had the townships of Middleton and Nesfield within it: Ilkley was in Skyrack wapentake and Middleton and Nesfield on the north side of the Wharfe were in Claro wapentake. In human terms, the wapentakes had importance as the units within which their inhabitants were taxed and called up for military services. The meeting point of a wapentake had importance for all the vills or townships lying within it because men from each vill had from time to time to attend the court of the wapentake to which they belonged. The meeting point for the men of Claro for example, was at Claro Hill near Allerton Mauleverer and that for Skyrack was at the Shire Oak, in modern Headingley.[9] The wapentake courts were, however, not as important as their hundred counterparts in southern and eastern England because many of the major privileges and responsibilities of administration lay with various feudal courts of the many honours and fees of the area. One wonders to what extent a Swaledale man ever thought of himself as a man of Richmondshire or as a man of Gilling West.

(d) Township

It was suggested in the first chapter that the physical nature of the Dales provided a natural basis upon which human activity could develop. If we assume that people with broadly similar needs and cultures settled the area then their demands from the land were similar. The clusters of settlers would choose places that offered some shelter, water and some useable land. Their need for land would depend also upon their style of

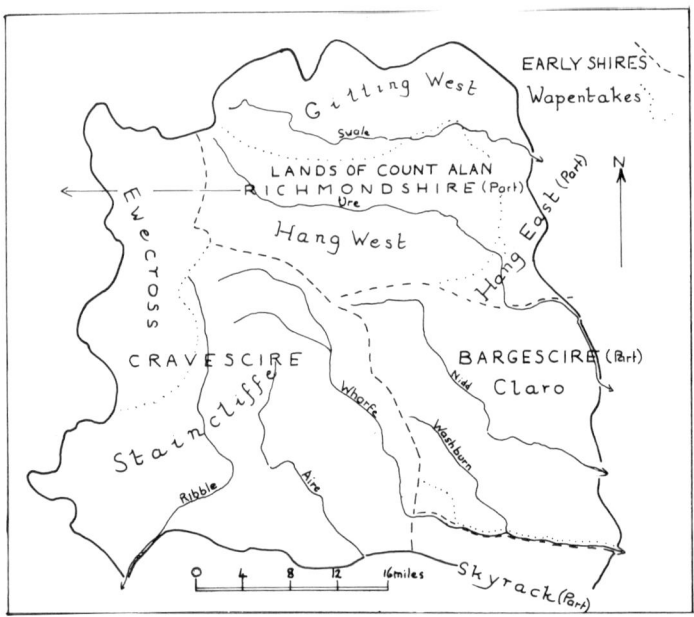

Fig. 14.   Political subdivisions of the Dales, 9th to 19th centuries.

farming, but it is reasonable to assume a need for grassland for cutting hay; a need for land upon which to grow crops and also for land from which fuel could be obtained; and finally a need for land on which stock could graze whilst the hay was growing. If stone suitable for building or good supplies of timber could be found so much the better. Groups of settlers would thus establish their townships with meadowland, cropland and moorland for communal use. As has been pointed out in the previous chapter, settlement came in a number of phases and by the time of the Norman Conquest the bulk of townships that we now see already existed, at least as the name of an area of land that may have undergone big changes since. As more permanent settlement replaced a scatter of communities, formal agreements had to be made over boundaries so that each community knew the limits of its common rights. It was most convenient if ridges or streams could be used: the ridges between valleys virtually always separated settlements. The map of a stretch of Littondale (fig. 15) illustrates this pattern very well. It also shows that compromises had to be reached between communities: Hawkswick township crosses the Skirfare whereas that of Arncliffe, perhaps with more useable and accessible land up Cowside Beck, occupied a typical valley site. Litton

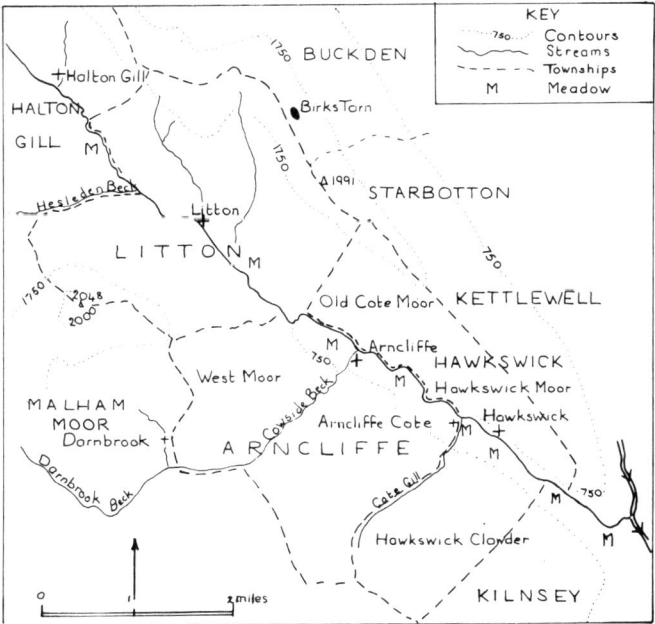

Fig. 15.   Littondale: Townships and boundaries.

31. Thors Dike, earthwork at head of Park Rash, looking south-west towards Great Whernside.

township, like Hawkswick, stretches watershed to watershed right across the valley. The boundaries between these settlements down the valley sides appear to be arbitrary in some cases, such as that between Hawkswick and Litton, and controlled by natural boundaries in others: Cote Beck makes an obviously convenient line between Arncliffe and Hawkswick to the south of the river. It is well worthwhile walking the bounds of a township in order to see if there are any physical reasons for its alignment on the ground and alternatively to see if man has himself set up key points such as large stones or even built banks better to define the limits of one community from another. The boundary between Kettlewell and Carlton Highdale (Coverdale) is a very striking earthwork called Thors Dike (photo 31). This dike, almost certainly already in existence, proved to be a valuable feature when township boundaries needed more exact definition.

The Church

Key events in the story of the evolution of the church in Northern England, which were of great importance for the later development of the area, took place in 661 A.D. when Wilfred brought the Benedictine system of monastic rule to Ripon and in 735 A.D. when the province of York was created. Earlier still in 601, Pope Gregory had ordered Augustine to establish a diocese at York with twelve bishops within the diocese. York thus became the focal point for the evolution of the organisations of the secular church in the North.

New dioceses gradually evolved that lay within the province of York: Durham replaced Lindisfarne as the seat of the Bishop of the North Coast in 995 A.D. A diocese known variously as Chester, Lichfield or Coventry was established after 1075 A.D. In 1133 King Henry I created the new diocese of Carlisle; it was defined as 'the territory of Dolphin— that is Carlisle and as much land as is geographically dependent on it'. It was increased, at the expense of the diocese of Chester, in 1856. In

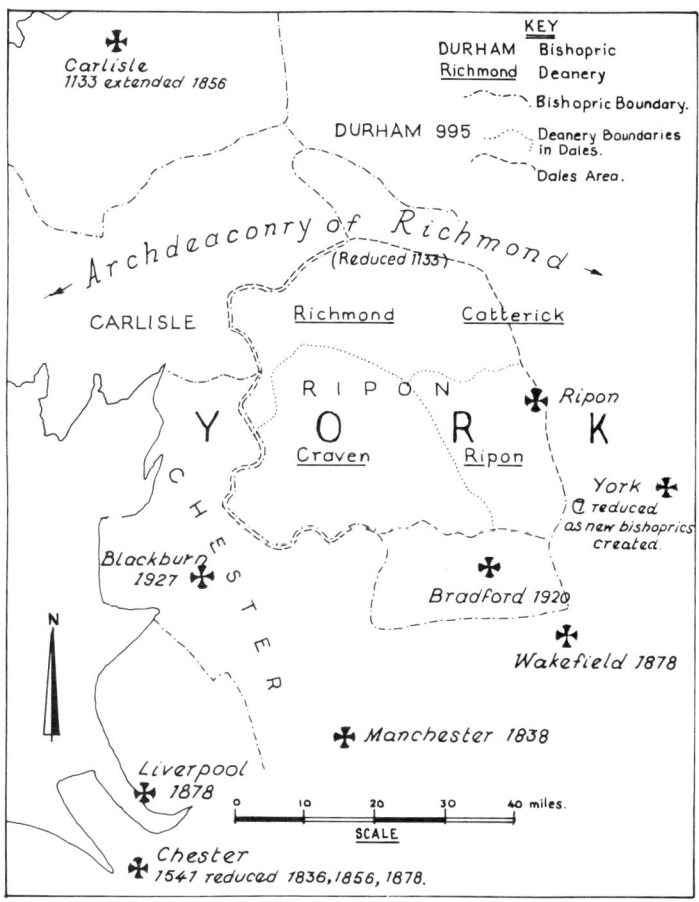

Fig. 16.   The organisation of the Church in North West England.

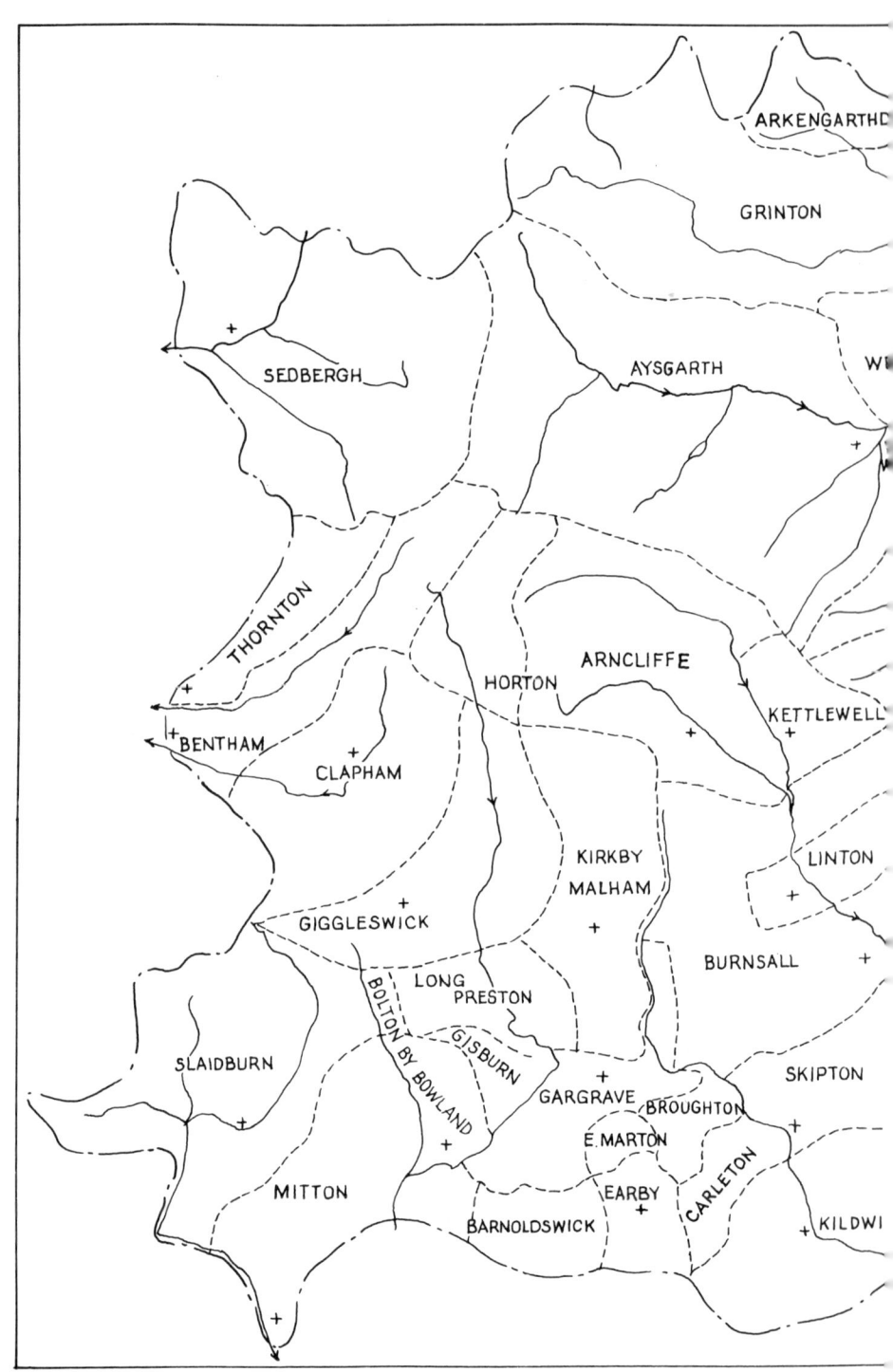

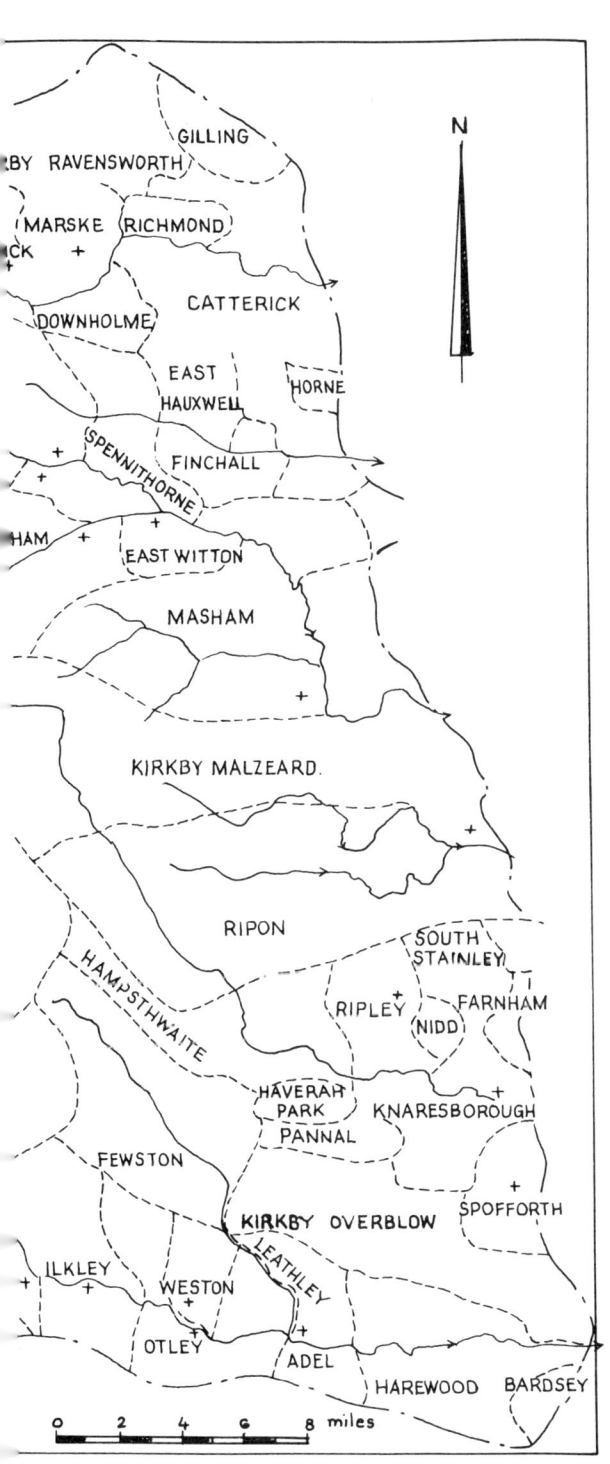

N

Fig. 17.   Ancient Parishes.

1541 Henry VIII created the new see of Chester, placing much of the huge archdeaconry of Richmond under its control and including the rural deaneries of Copeland, Furness, Cartmel, Kirkby Lonsdale and Kendal under the wing of the new bishop.

As the new bishoprics were created, the see of York was reduced but the primacy of York remained. The remainder of Yorkshire outside the new bishopric, therefore, lay entirely within the diocese of the archbishop, so that it was essential that the huge area was subdivided for many matters of church organisation. The day to day work of running the diocese was carried out by four archdeacons. The archdeaconry of Richmond which preceded and survived the creations of Carlisle and Chester dioceses had an enormous area of responsibility, originally stretching over all the deaneries of what was to become Cumberland, Westmorland and North Lancashire as well as north-west Yorkshire. The creation of the bishoprics of Chester and Durham reduced the tributary area and the archdeaconry became co-terminous with the western half of the North Riding after 1133. The central west part of the West Riding was under the authority of the archdeacon of York.

Church organisation was modified further in 1836 when the Dales area was very nearly made co-terminous with the newly created bishopric of Ripon. The Yorkshire part of the archdeaconry of Richmond came to Ripon as did all the deanery of Craven and parts of the Ainsty and of Pontefract deaneries. The Archbishop of York thus ceased to have other than primate powers within the area.

Four archdeaconries were still very large areas for the archdeacons in the see of York to control and rural deaneries were established for the day to day running of groups of parishes. These were earlier units than might be expected, having been set up by the twelfth century. The relationship of the deaneries to the area of the Dales, like that of so many other human patterns, is that places giving their names to the deaneries are marginal to their tributary areas. Richmond had a rural dean as well as its archdeacon: Catterick and Boroughbridge both on the edge of the Plain of York also became head churches of deaneries. The rural deanery of Craven continued the name of what has already been shown to be a very ancient unit in the history of the area and it and the rural deanery of the City and Ainsty of York both lay in the archdeaconry of York and later in the archdeaconry of Ripon.

The term parish has been avoided so far in describing the organisation of the settlements in the Dales, where groups of people either settled in

Church style in the Dales. **32** (top left). The Norman tower, Masham. **33** (top right). Norman simplicity—the chancel at Conistone, Wharfedale. **34** (bottom left). 15th century architecture at Kirkby Malham, and **35** (bottom right) detail of same.

or gradually cohered into townships. The settlements only became parishes in the ecclesiastical sense later in their history. The present organisation of civil parishes stems from the pattern of ecclesiastical parishes which existed in 1888 when the Local Government Act creating County Councils, Rural Districts and Civil Parishes was passed.

Parish churches are key buildings in many Dales townships. In some, the existence of a church has been significant in part of the naming of the place; for example, Kirkby Malham, Kirkby Malzeard and Kirkby Overblow (photos 34, 35). In a number of parishes the survival of the ruins of an abbey or priory reminds us that the monastic system was of great importance until the Dissolution of the Monasteries. In all these ways, church organisation and history has exercised an influence on what we now see in the Dales and upon the way in which various aspects of their government and social structure are organised.

A major contrast between the south-east and the north-west of England is to be found in the way in which ecclesiastical parish structure has evolved. In south-east England nearly every township and often manor had its own church. A pattern of small parishes, averaging perhaps, one thousand acres evolved. In the Dales and Cumbria, the reverse happened. A parish church was founded and much of a dale was thus served by the one church: this happened at Arncliffe in Littondale and Muker in Swaledale for example. Despite the devastation of the north by William I, Norman churches were built in and around the Dales. Norman elements are to be seen at Addingham, Adel (near Leeds), Leatheley, Guiseley, Linton in Craven, Thornton in Lonsdale (ruined by fire in 1933), Sedbergh, Dent, Kirkby Malzeard, Knaresborough, St. Mary Richmond, Masham, Coniston (Wharfedale), Horton-in-Ribblesdale, Gisburn, Grinton, Marton, Bracewell, Broughton, Farnham, Marske, West Witton, Wensley, Gilling, Downholme, St. Oswald Hauxwell (late eleventh century), Patrick Brompton, Hornby, Finghall and Spennithorne.[10, 12] It is clear that many of the 'old' parishes must have existed at the time of the Conquest. It is also clear that a good deal of Norman rebuilding must have taken place fairly quickly after William I had laid the area waste. The development of some ecclesiastical parishes is a puzzle: Dent lay within the parish of Sedbergh, yet its church has Norman elements; Ingleton lay within the medieval parish of Bentham, yet it too had an early medieval church, if its Norman font is indigenous, although Speight refers to Ingleton church as a parochial chapel to Bentham.[13] Horton-in-Ribblesdale church has much surviving Norman work—'in some respects this is the most interesting church in Craven, for we have an almost complete nave of late Norman work and a south doorway of the same period'.[14]

When looking at the existing churches of the Dales it must be remembered that much rebuilding has taken place, especially in the nineteenth century. Kettlewell had a small Norman church, but as Shuffrey noted, it was pulled down in 1819 and 'in its place a plain long edifice was erected without any regard to beauty or elegance. It had square wooden sash windows and a white-washed ceiling extending the whole length'.[15] Pevsner notes that the present building, apart from the tower, dates from a further restoration in 1882–5. In general, Shuffrey pointed out that little Norman work survives in Craven churches and that it is the reigns of Henry VII, Henry VIII and Victoria that contributed most to their appearance.

The term 'ancient' parish is itself an arbitrary one. It is probable, for example, that Burnsall parish was a sub-division of a bigger and older parish of Linton. Shuffrey noted that one third of Burnsall's corn tithe went to Linton and this is a typical tithe arrangement when a new parish is taken out of an earlier one.[16] The ancient ecclesiastical parishes proved to be too large and inconvenient as the population of the Dales gradually increased. The long treks to the parish church for those who were to be married or the journeys of parents to baptise their children and of relations to bury their dead, proved difficult and disagreeable. Chapels of Ease were established in the more isolated parts of ancient parishes; for example, one was built at Toss-side in Gisburn Forest as a chapel within Gisburn parish. In 1771 this chapel was in ruins and a brief was issued for £1,189 for repairs; a new ecclesiastical parish of Toss-side was created in 1870. Whitaker, writing of the rapid growth of churches in the Leeds area, was not in favour of the new ones that were being built; he commented that 'the duration of an early Norman church may be contrasted with the deformity, the frailty, and the tasteless expense of many modern ecclesiastical buildings which, as they have sprung up in the present generation, will scarcely propagate the memory of its bad taste beyond the next'.

New churches were built for new parishes and obviously most of these were in areas of population growth—in Harrogate, for example, a run of nineteenth century churches was built. Ancient parishes such as Long Preston were subdivided into several new parishes: Hellifield's church was not built until as late as 1905, and Settle in the neighbouring ancient parish of Giggleswick was provided with its own parish church in the early nineteenth century.

New networks of church, or more correctly, chapel-going became evident from the early seventeenth century as non-conformity developed, at times very strongly, in the Dales. Quaker chapels, such as that at Brigflatts near Sedbergh, dated 1675, became very important local centres for members of the new religious groups. The Quakers established a Meeting House at Skipton in 1693 and the history of non-conformity can be clearly followed by the record of church building in Skipton. The Congregationalists built their first chapel there in 1777 and rebuilt it in 1860. The Wesleyan Methodists built in 1811 and then built a new chapel in 1865; the Primitive Methodists also progressed in two stages, 1835 and 1870. In 1836 the Roman Catholics built their own church and the Baptists, building in 1871, were followed by the United Methodists. Under the pressure of population growth a second Anglican parish, that of Christ Church, was created in 1839 to cope with the western part of the ancient parish of Skipton.[17] Each of these sects contributed a new element to the urban and social fabric of Skipton as indeed they did to many of the villages of the Dales as a whole.

The Feudal System

The Norman Conquest had a third important effect on the region, which was additional to the development of a system of national government and a system of ecclesiastical organisation. This was the imposition of the feudal system on to the social fabric. William I re-allotted most of the land of the region to his followers. Some estates such as those of the Archbishop of York or those of the canons of Ripon already existed, but land held by Saxon thegns or by Danes was redistributed to loyal Normans. Sub-infeudation then took place, especially to the newly-founded monastic houses and to lesser Norman families. Compound place names give us some clue to these events. In making a major land grant the Norman kings

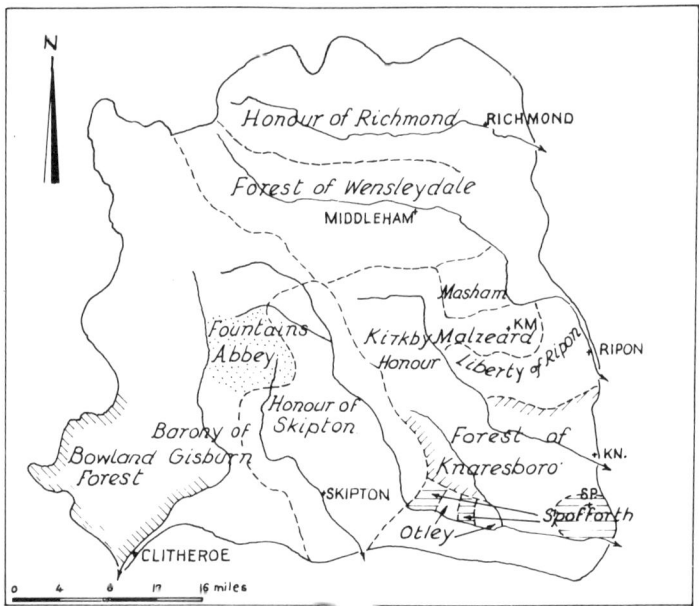

Fig. 18.   Major feudal units in the Dales (based on R. B. Smith, 'Lordships of the West Riding', 1835, Map 3.

granted their tenants in chiefs very considerable powers and the lands over which these powers could be exercised were known as at Skipton as an Honour or in the case of the grant to the Percy family as a Fee. In other cases the privileges were described as extending within a Liberty, as in the case of Ripon. The patterns of jurisdiction changed as families came into or fell out of favour with the monarch and also became extremely complex.

It is difficult now to know what the significance was to the local inhabitants of living in one of these feudal units; the Honour of Richmond, for example. In practical terms it may have determined from whom permission was sought for felling timber, or as to where a house might be built and how many many stock might be kept: it almost certainly determined to which court malefactors for a wide range of offences were brought. The main centre of a tenant-in-chief's lands, be it Richmond, Ripon or Kirkby Malzeard, was bound to become relatively important: often a market was established and perhaps fairs as well. In 1387 the Nevilles for example secured a market charter for Middleham and in 1251 Alan Fitz Alan received authority to hold a market at Bedale.

The greatest single land grant of the region was that made by William I to Count Alan; this was known as the Honour of Richmond or sometimes Richmondshire. It was a grant which gave considerable powers to the grantee so that a buffer could be provided against Scottish invasion (the boundary of Scotland lay in Stainmore in the twelfth century). Richmond-shire survived with its own courts until the seventeenth century. The Honour was one which reverted several times to the Crown and was given to Royal Dukes by various monarchs; its major surviving importance latterly, was for titles to the lead workings in Swaledale.

The Honour of Skipton was an important unit in the medieval organisation of the region. Fig. 19 shows the approximate extent of the Honour as recorded in the period 1284–1314. This Honour grew in importance with the fortunes of the Percy family and the building of the castle at Skipton from which their estates were run was a major contribution to the growth of the town. Roads from Skipton into Wharfedale, to Bolton Abbey and to Barden, must have been very busy from 1300 onwards as the many aspects of life in the area were carried out and goods were brought from outlying parts of the Fee.

In the east of the Dales, the Liberty of Ripon originated as a grant of land in 661 A.D. to St. Wilfred by Alchfrith, a Northumbrian prince. When the Archbishopric of York was created the Liberty was divided between the archbishop and the chapter of Ripon. The latter was granted estates within the Liberty which included nearly half of Ripon burgh in 1228 and lands in almost all the townships in the manor. For example they held one third of the manor of Mulwith and six tofts and nine acres in Grantley and Eaviston. In addition, each prebend had specific endowments, e.g. the prebend of Monkton was endowed with lands in Monkton that

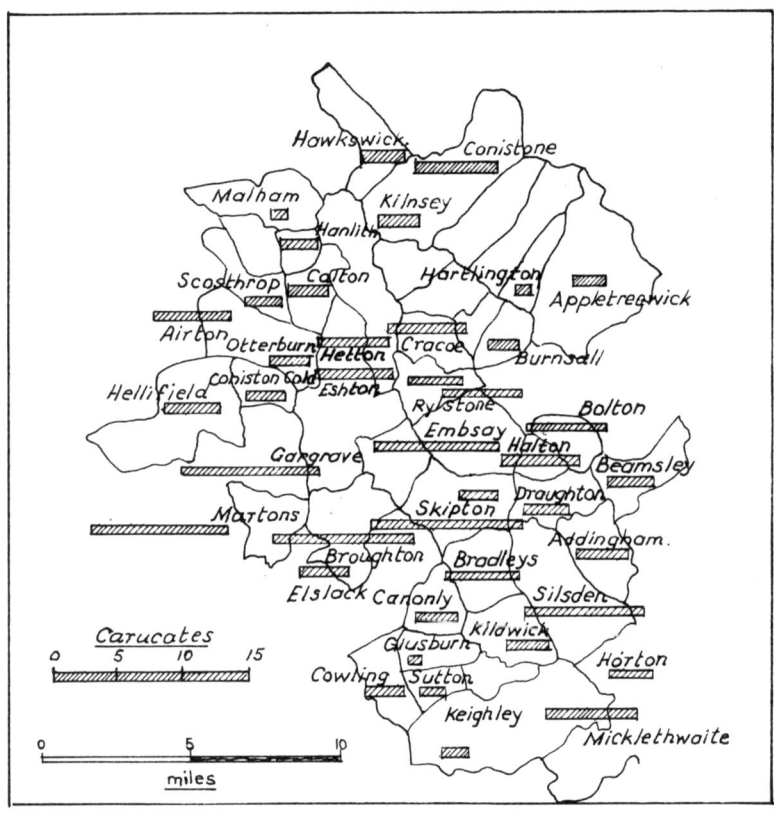

Fig. 19. The Honour of Skipton, 1284–1314 A.D.

would support a residentiary canon. As mentioned earlier, the chapter of
Ripon held strong ecclesiastical powers within the parish of Ripon.

The archbishop's Liberty was coincidental with the great manor of Ripon
and a number of tributary manors lay within the principal manor; these
secondary manors were held by laymen and were originally the means
by which the knight service would be provided to the archbishop and by
the archbishop (as a laylord) to the king. In 1545 the rental of the manor
was given as £143.0.0 per annum. The archbishop held several courts
within the Liberty and in 1285–1298 Archbishop John Romaine claimed
and was allowed very wide powers.

In 1319 Pateley Bridge, lying in Bishopdale (the Bishop's side) was granted a market charter by King Edward II to Archbishop William Melton. The Liberty accepted responsibility for the repair of bridges within its boundaries. Many of the powers of the feudal landowners together with many of those of modern local government resided in the hands of the Archbishop (or his Steward) acting as a powerful lay figure. The names of these parishes—Bishopside, Bishop Monkton and Bishop Thornton—and the existence of Pateley Bridge as an important centre all bear witness to the impact that the original ancient land grant to St. Wilfred had on events many centuries later. This original grant ensured that a thriving market city would develop at Ripon.

References

[1] P. Hunter Blair, *Roman Britain and Early England 55 B.C.–871 A.D.*, London 1963.

[2] *Handbook of British Chronology*, Royal Historical Society, 1961, p.26.

[3] R. Alken Brown, *The Normans and the Norman Conquest*, London 1969, p.75.

[4] *V.C.H. Yorkshire*, Vol. 3, p.395.

[5] as above, p.394.

[6] Elgee, p.204.

[7] North Yorkshire V.C.H.-I, p.419.

[8] H. C. Darby and J. S. Maxwell, *The Domesday Geography of Northern England*, Cambridge 1962, figs. 2 and 21.

[9] G. R. J. Jones, *Multiple Estates and Early Settlement in Medieval Settlement*, Ed. Sawyer, London, 1976.

[10] H. Speight, *Upper Wharfedale*, London 1900, p.43.

[11] H. Speight, *Romantic Richmondshire*, London 1897, p.335.

[12] N. Pevsner, *The Buildings of England: Yorkshire West Riding*, London 1959.

[13] as above, *North Riding*, London 1966.

[14] W. A. Shuffrey, *North Craven Churches*, Leeds 1914 (hereafter Shuffrey), p.236.

[15] Shuffrey, p.41.

[16] Shuffrey, p.49.

[17] 'The Honour of Skipton 1284–1314'. E.Y.C., Vol. 7, Y.R.S. Extra Series, Vol. 5, 1947.

5

Settlement Patterns

THE traveller in the Yorkshire Dales must quickly be struck by the attractive clusters of buildings, usually on the lower valley slopes and often protected by a maze of stone walls and clumps of ash and sycamore trees. A mixture of farmsteads, hamlets, villages and market towns is scattered, in the main along the lower valley sides in the upper dales, but more evenly as the dales open out to the surrounding lowlands. Fig. 20 shows a typical valley settlement pattern.

The least complex element of the pattern is that of the farmstead: a group of buildings concerned entirely with making a living from the land. The limestone, sandstones and grits provided a plentiful supply of building stones and these stones gave to the buildings a textural link with the physical landscapes in which they were set. As well as the dwellinghouse there are usually barns, sometimes built as an extension of the house, cattle stalls and other storage buildings. Next to the buildings are lambing enclosures and dipping pens and one or two walled lanes leading from the buildings to the surrounding fields.

The stone farmhouses often carry datestones and these frequently bear a late seventeenth century date. Hoskins has termed this phase of stone farmhouse building the 'great rebuild'. In all probability these stone farmhouses have replaced timber buildings, perhaps of the cruck type. In areas that were forest or chase until after the Dissolution it may be that the buildings were stone-built from the start but in the hamlets and villages that existed in 1086 timber, wattle and clay were probably the main building materials.

Walton, Barley and R. F. Taylor all discuss the cruck house in Yorkshire and North Lancashire.[1 3] Walton describes the surviving cruck buildings in Wharfedale: in some cases stone gables had a cruck in order to make a two-bay house. Taylor refers to an accepted tradition in medieval Wales that a man had a right to three timbers from a wood, the three being the ridge and the two crucks. Barley quotes Whitaker writing about Whalley parish (Lancashire) in 1801 as pointing out that many cottages in Whalley were 'Single apartments without chambers, open to their thatched roofs and supported upon crucks'. A late sixteenth century survey, quoted by Barley referring to the Craco and Silsden areas, makes reference to oak being used as well as ash and elm to make and repair their ancient firehouses and barns.[4] Nicholas Ricroft was described as having built 'one firehouse and a lath of three pair of crucks and one kiln'; Richard Cookson had built a 'firehouse of four pairs of crucks—oak'. He also had a barn and a hay house, each of two pairs of crucks. Most of the buildings referred to in this late sixteenth century survey were of three bays and one only had an upper floor. Taylor suggests that a cruck building near Kirkham, Lancashire, was built in the late seventeenth century with wattle walls. The buildings shown in the photographs at Hubberholme are probably late seventeenth and early eighteenth century in date (photo 36). Ingthorpe Grange carries late seventeenth century dates on the porch: the windows may well be modified, especially those in the end gable (photos 37, 38).

Hamlets can be regarded as the second tier of a settlement sequence and they usually represent small groups of farms, concentrated at a good site, but they may also reflect a small settlement resulting from some additional activity such as mining or the existence of a smithy. Halton Gill,

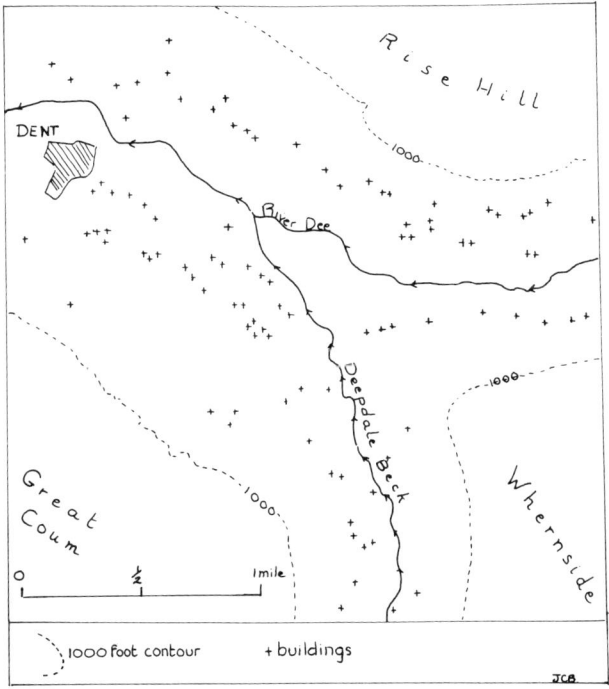

Fig. 20.   The settlement pattern in Dentdale.

36. The 'long house' type – two farmhouses with barns at Hubberholme, Upper Wharfedale. **37.** Ingthorpe Grange, Martons, Craven. Manor/farmhouse with porch date 1671 and 1672. **38.** Barn and yards at Ingthorpe Grange. **39, 40** (this page). Farms and manor house at Halton Gill.

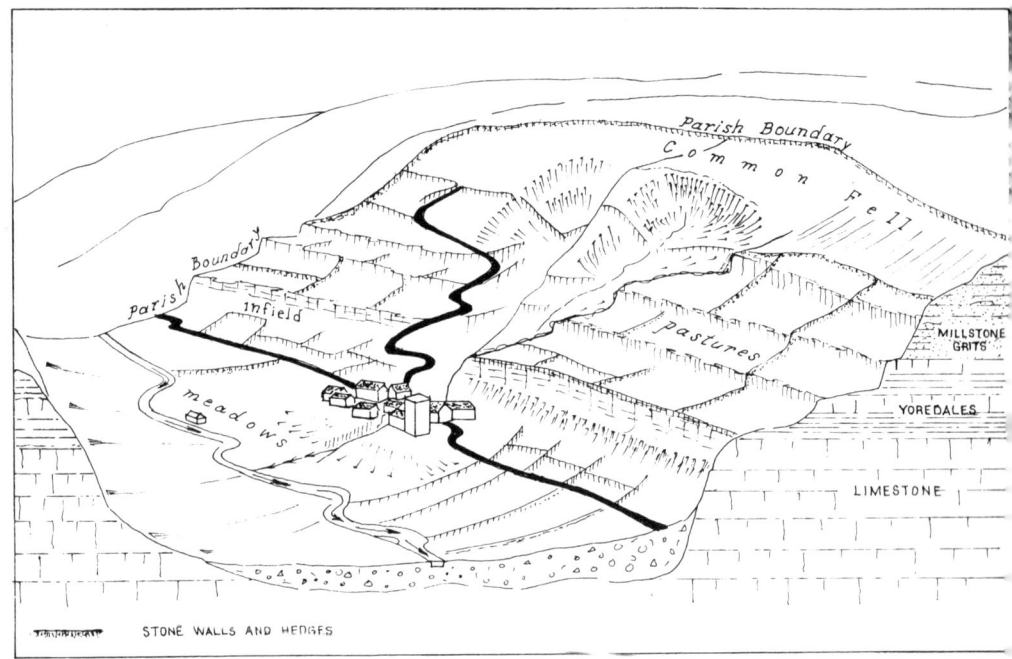

Fig. 21. A Dales Parish.
Opposite: Arncliffe village. **41.** South side of the green. **42.** East end of the green. **43.** The bridge—an important element in many villages.

tucked away at the head of Littondale, is a good example of such a small hamlet and consists of a fine group of stone-built farmsteads: probably all of the late seventeenth century (photo 39). Notice the typical longhouse in the upper photograph, and the double range 'manor house' with large porch in the lower photograph (photo 40). In 1801 Halton Gill had 139 people, in 1971 it had 35: so it is perhaps more accurately described as a once small village that has now become a hamlet. The little church was rebuilt in 1848, having previously been rebuilt as a chapel in 1636. Other small scattered settlements have tended to decline in a way similar to Halton Gill. Coverdale had 398 people in 1821 but only a quarter of this total by 1971. Coverdale was a collection of farmsteads given unity by their lying in the same small dale rather than as hamlets of grouped buildings.

The village is at the third level in the range of settlement types. Arncliffe in Littondale (photos 41–43), Starbottom in Wharfedale, West Burton in Wensleydale, are good examples of the true village. Fig. 21 shows a typical

dales village layout. Its water supply comes from a tributary stream and the small tributary valley may also provide some shelter. The village will be a little above the level of the main river valley floor in case of flooding. Farms, one or two inns, a church, a non-conformist chapel, a school, two or three shops, the smithy-turned-garage and a water-mill all combine to make a focal point for the isolated farms or hamlets up and down dale.

Writing perhaps part descriptively and part with nostalgia Whitaker, praising Richmondshire, says of its villages 'that manufactures have scarcely made an inroad upon its borders, many of [the village] surround spacious greens and a vast elm frequently marks the place where the sports of the young and and the conferences of the aged have taken place for centuries'.[5] He takes a swipe at his hated manufactories in his comments on other villages: Burley-in-Wharfedale he describes as 'a delightful village, though contaminated physically and morally by a cotton mill'. The villages were in many cases changing in character quite noticeably by the end of the eighteenth century. He was however, able to praise Bolton-by-

44 (opposite top). Bolton by Bowland – church and village.   **45** (this page). Reeth, showing the village green (Cambridge University Collection).   **46** (opposite bottom). Masham market place – perhaps a former green.

Bowland: 'this and some adjoining parishes still continue to prove the good effects produced by extensive properties in preventing the introduction of manufactures, those hot-beds of early immorality, premature marriage and unnatural population. It is to be hoped that the eyes of every nobleman and gentleman in the kingdom will speedily be opened to the real nature of these gigantic pests'.[6]

An important element in many of the Wensleydale villages in particular and in the villages bordering the Vale of York is that of the green. Thorpe studied the green villages of County Durham in detail and he tentatively concluded that they may have originated as 'defensive enclosures established on naturally open sites, often small in extent, in formerly forested country'. He suggested that they were probably Anglian in origin but that it was by no means clear whether they were the original settlement forms.[7] He recognised broad greens, street greens and greens of indefinite shape. Reeth in Swaledale (photo 45) is an excellent example of the first category and

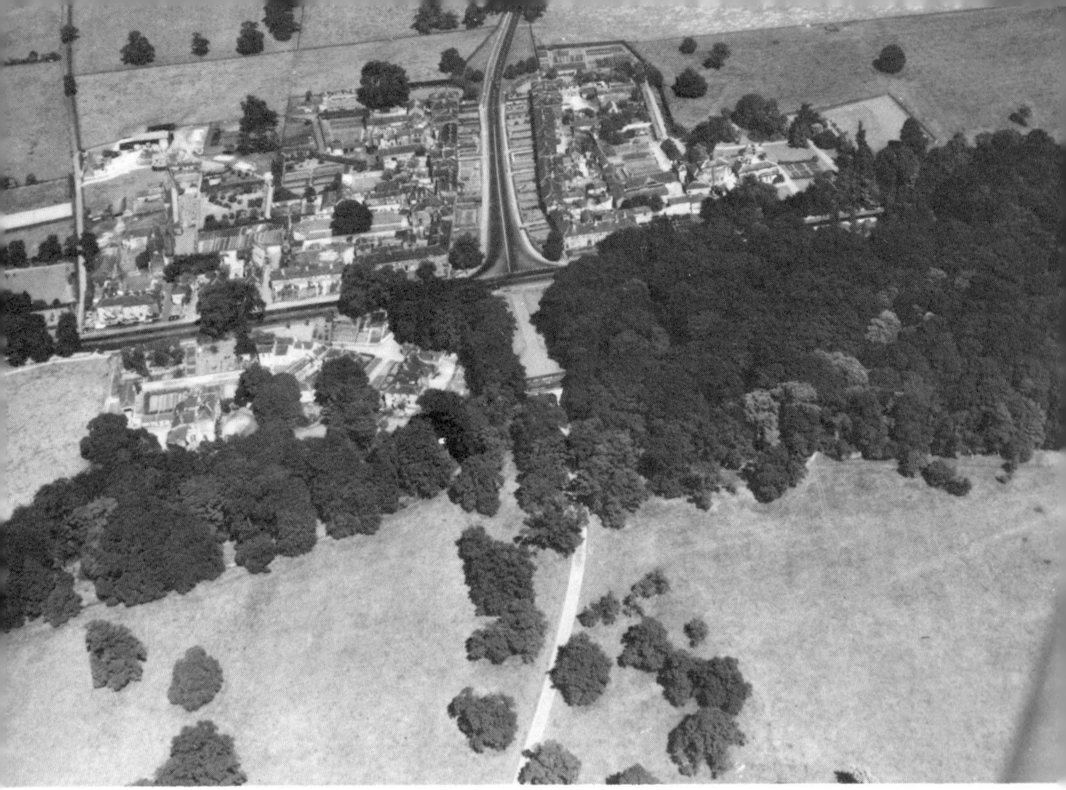

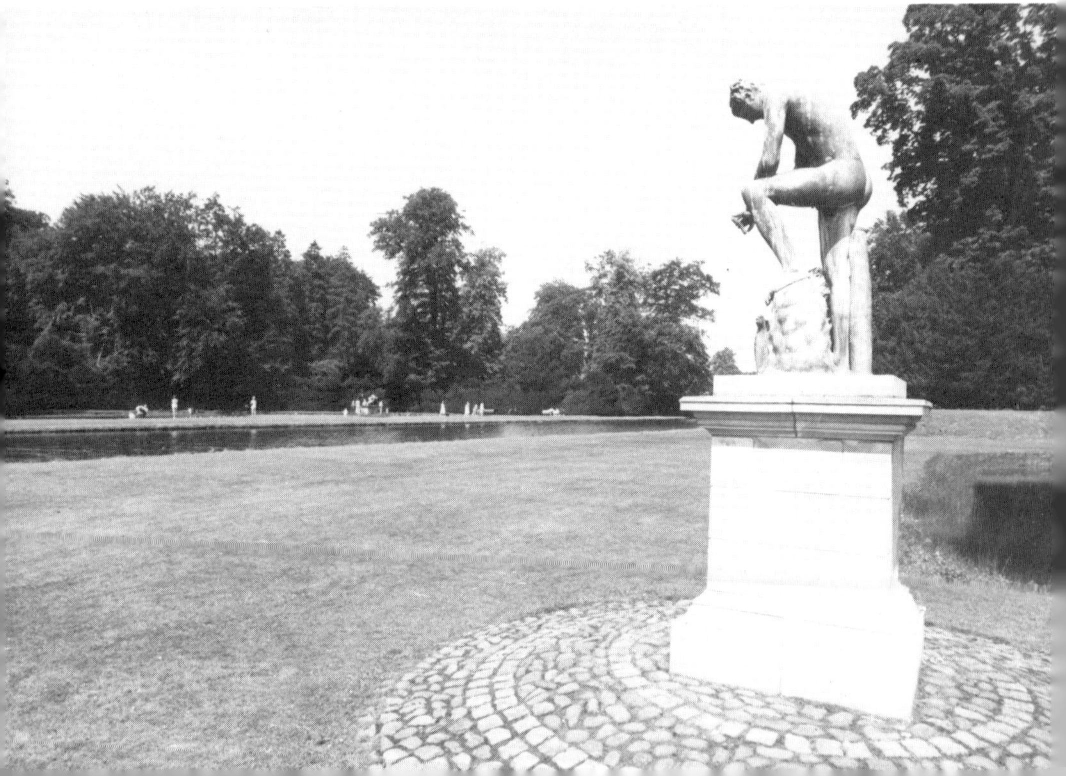

in lower Wensleydale a number of villages show this form; East Witton is an especially good example of a street green. Thorpe also pointed out that the green villages of Durham were on the whole, the bigger villages and this seems a valied observation in the Dales also. Indeed some of the green villages may have evolved into the market towns of the post Norman period such as Masham with its huge market place (photo 46) or Bedale with its triangular market place. Much remains to be discovered about the original shapes and the later changing shapes of the green villages because Norman and Scottish devastations combined with the influence of wealthy church and lay landowners may have led to the near disappearance of some, followed perhaps, by a later rekindling of communities in quite new forms.

An additional element that became an increasingly significant part of the landscape during the latter part of the seventeenth century and especially during the eighteenth was that of the 'gentleman's seat'. The dissolution of the monasteries, as has already been pointed out, led to a massive redistribution of lands. Those who bought were often lawyers who were doing well, or merchants who were prospering from one or other branch of the textile trade. Lower Wharfedale was near to Leeds, a major market of the cloth industry, and wealth began to flow back to some estates and to allow successful enterpreneurs to buy up others. Once bought, they vied with one another to landscape them. At Harewood, Henry Lascelles, a ribbon merchant, bought the Cowthorpe estate for his son. John Carr designed the house and Robert Adam worked on the interior, and at a cost of £16,000 Capability Brown laid out the park. As so often happened, the main road—the Skipton–Knaresborough turnpike—was diverted from the park and an attractive new estate village designed by John Carr was laid out at the gate (photo 47). The striking ruins of the thirteenth century castle overlook Wharfedale and the old Gowthorpe Hall lies in the park to the south-west of the present Harewood House.

Other Wharfedale estates that bear the stamp of eighteenth century architecture and landscaping are those of Farnley, Weston, Denton and Bolton Abbey. The tree planting on estates in the Ribble valley has already been mentioned. In the Richmond area large estates were laid out at, for example, Aske to the north of Richmond where an early 'pele' tower of the Aske family was incorporated into later buildings by the Wharton and Dundas (Marquis of Zetland) families. Again, Capability Brown is known to have worked on the park, which had a Gothic temple, and Oliver's Ducket (a rebuilt tower from Richmond Castle) was used to

47. Harewood – the new village laid out by John Carr in 1760 for Edwin Lascelles. **48.** Statuary in the water gardens at Studley Royal (Clifford Robinson).

complete the landscape improvements.[8,9] Another area of splendid land-scaping was the park of Studley Royal which was laid out by John Aislabie in the 1720s. Vanbrugh's new house has since been demolished. The park, later linked to the Fountains Estate by John Aislabie's son William, survives as a perfect piece of improved landscape with its exotic trees, canals, fountains and temples (photo 48).[10]

The landscape improvements of the major landed families were echoed by the squirearchy and often by the clergy too: new facades were added to earlier farm houses, new rectories were built and small parks laid out around them. Many very interesting early buildings were modified and on a considerable scale too: Guiseley Rectory for example, an original medieval aisled hall, was improved in 1601 by a wealthy rector.[11] As Barley points out the immediately recognisable regional style of building gradually gave way to other classical styles of the seventeenth and eighteenth centuries: pillared, pedimented, symmetrical buildings, standing supreme in their parks at the head of avenues of oaks, limes and elm trees became an important part of the rural landscape (photos 49–51).[12]

Market Towns

Around the edge of the Dales and in most cases outside the Yorkshire Dales National Park lie the market towns upon which the upper valleys focus for their trade. The actual siting of these towns was often the result of strategic considerations, the castles of Skipton, Knaresborough and Richmond for example. But once the defensive sites were established markets followed, for example Knaresborough's market was first mentioned in 1206. These markets lay at the meeting point between the dales, with their surplus stock and wool, and the plain with its surplus corn. It also helped the growth of a market if it lay at the centre of a particular group of family possessions; Skipton was the centre of an important Fee held by the Cliffords. Manor Courts would meet at the castle; fairs were held several times a year; the mill was often one of the Lord's possessions. A variety of economic and social activities evolved around castle and market, or as at Ripon around Minster and market. In the later Middle Ages and into the modern period, Quarter Sessions would meet in these towns; workhouses were built, barracks established, the seats of local government, town halls and assembly rooms were built. Finally, these towns were further strengthened by the construction of better roads to improve trade, by the development of canals as at Skipton and Ripon, and by the construction of railways. Gas works and waterworks proved essential. In nearly all the old market towns, grammar schools were endowed for the education of the local children in Latin, Greek, English grammar and the Catechism, as at Knaresborough when Mr. Benson founded the school in 1616.[13]

The air photograph and the map of Ripon (photo 52, fig. 22) clearly illustrate the main points in the structure of this market town. The original

The 17th century rebuild in the Dales. **49** (top left). Surviving porch of 17th century manor house at Threshfield. **50** (top right). Late 17th/early 18th century classical influence at Thorpe. **51.** Kirkby Malham vicarage – the porch is dated 1622.

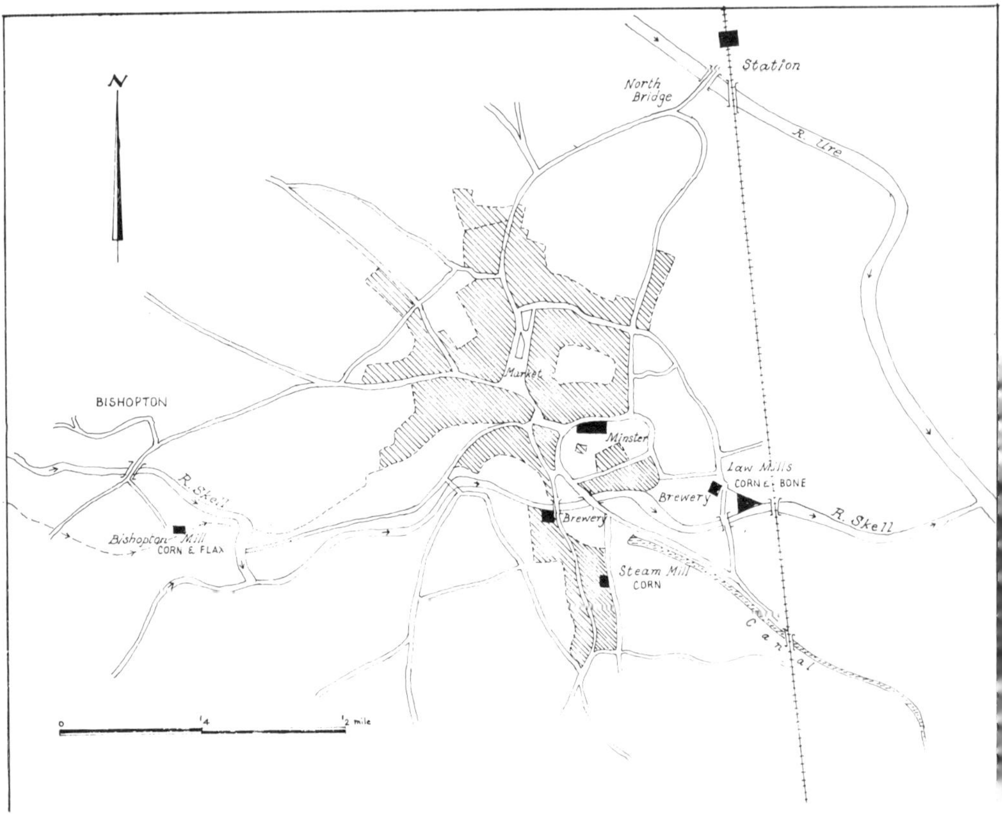

N

BISHOPTON

R. Skell

Bishopton Mill
CORN & FLAX

Market

Minster

Brewery

Brewery

Steam Mill
CORN

North
Bridge

Station

R. Ure

Tow Mills
CORN & BONE

R. Skell

Canal

0   ¼   ½ mile

site lay between the rivers Skell and Ure and it must have attracted
Saint Wilfrid either because of the existence of some settlement already
there or because of the upstanding nature of the dry, protected spur of
land on which to build his early church. Thereafter, under the protection
of the Archbishop of York, the rebuilt Minster, which was the focal point
of the Liberty of Ripon, together with the market flourished. The air
photograph looks southwards to the bridge across the Skell. Celia Fiennes
noted 'there are two good bridges to the town, one was a rebuilding
pretty large with several arches called Hewet [Hewick] Bridge is often out
of repair by reason of the force of the water that swells after great
raines, yet I see they make works of wood on purpose to break the violence
of the streame and the middle arch is very large and high.'[14] The
impressive Minster, now a cathedral, stands high above this crossing;
the market place lies north of the Minster. The property boundaries run
away at right angles to the line of the market place and the mixture of
periods and functions of buildings that overlooks the market combines to
produce the architectural variety that is so typical of English market towns.
As a market, Ripon grew under the encouragement and patronage of the
archbishop of York: Henry I granted a market charter to the archbishop
in 1108 A.D. The church not only held the market rights; the Canons of
Ripon owned much of the land in the town, and Fountains Abbey also
held some property there. There were three medieval hospitals, two bridge
chapels and a grammar school all adding to the important religious life
of the medieval town.[15]

Richmond is by far the most important place at the north-east corner
of the Dales (photo 53). The importance of Richmondshire or the Honour
of Richmond has already been mentioned. From Richmond the Honour
was administered and to Richmond physical geography focused all the
trade to and from Swaledale. Speight gave an excellent account of Richmond
and he summarised its character in the nineteenth century as follows:
'In addition to the Castle and its belongings there are two very ancient
churches, several monasteries, chapels, chantries, crosses, guilds, colleges,
schools and hospitals besides other secular and religious institutions, now
or in past times existing, lying within or about the town.'[16]

Count Alan, to whom William I gave Richmondshire, began to build the
castle at Richmond after 1071. There was no previous settlement of any
importance on this site; it appears that Gilling and Catterick had been
the earlier more important places. It seems odd now, in view of the superbly
sited castle, that Richmond was a completely new Norman town. The

52. Ripon, looking south (Cambridge University Collection).   Fig. 22. Ripon in 1857 (based on
1st edition O.S. 6″ sheet, CXIX, NW and NE).

market place occupies the original outer bailey of the castle, and markets were held in it. Burgage plots of the new town were probably laid out around this outer bailey but within the area enclosed by the town walls. The market flourished partly to serve the castle and partly because of its protection. In between 1136 and 1145, an important grant was made to the burgesses giving them freedom to run their own affairs in return for an annual rental of £29. This really created a self-governing 'borough' and further encouraged the growth of the town.

Speight quotes a fourteenth century grant by King Edward II of tolls to be levied on good sold in the market in order to maintain the walls. This list gives a vivid picture of the wildlife and the economy of the area. In particular it reflects the great importance of the various aspects of the wool and cloth trade in the first decade of the fourteenth century:

> For every eight bushels of corn was taken one halfpenny.
> For every horse, mare, ox, and cow, one halfpenny.
> For every hide of horse, mare, ox, and cow, fresh, salted or tanned, one farthing.
> For every cart-load of salted or fresh meat, three halfpence.

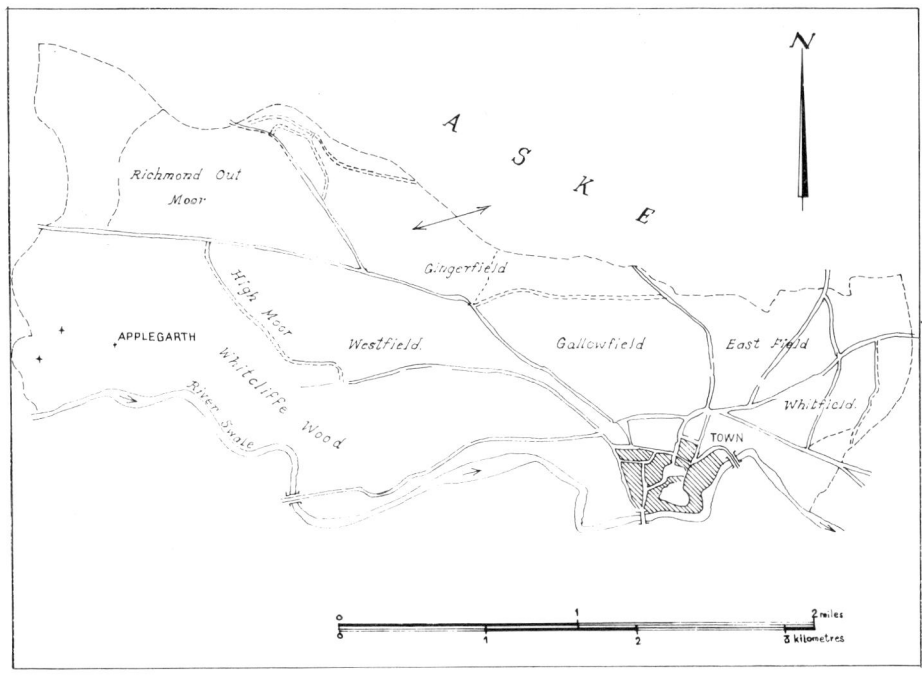

53. Richmond, looking west (Cambridge University Collection). Fig. 23. The Fields of Richmond.

For five fat hogs, one halfpenny.

For every salmon, fresh or salted, one farthing.

For every hundred mulnells conger and stikar eels (some kinds of dried fish from the North Sea) salted, one penny.

For every hundred skins of sheep shorn, goats, stags, hinds, bucks and does, one halfpenny.

For ten sheep, goats or pigs, one penny.

For ten fleeces, one penny.

For every hundred skins of lambs, kids, hares, rabbits, foxes, cats and squirrels, one halfpenny.

For every hundred (each containing one hundred ells, and every hundred ells six score) of linen web, canvas, Irish cloth, Galewith and Worstead, one penny.

For every horseload of cloth, one halfpenny.

For every shole piece of cloth, one halfpenny.

For every piece of silken cloth without gold, and chef (ten ells) of sendal imported, one farthing.

For every lamprey sold before the Passover, one halfpenny.

For every tun of wine and potashes, three halfpence.

For every horseload of hones, one penny.

For every tun of honey, two pence.

For every sack (twenty-six stone) of wool, two pence.
For every truss of cloth brought in a cart, two pence.
For every horseload of cloth or of divers other minute articles coming to the town, one halfpenny.
For every cartload of iron, one penny.
For every horseload of iron, one halfpenny.
For every cartload of lead, two pence.
For every cartload of tan to be sold during the week, one penny.
For every quarter of woad, two pence.
For eight sheaves of garlic, one farthing.
For every thousand herrings, one halfpenny.
For every horseload of sea fish, one halfpenny.
For every hundred boards, one halfpenny.
For every quarter (eight bushels) of salt, one farthing.
For every weigh (fourteen stone) of cheese and butter, one halfpenny.
For every cartload of brushwood or coals in the weekdays, one halfpenny.
For every thousand faggots, one penny.
For every weigh of tallow and lard, one penny.[17]

In the sixteenth century, though linen remained important, it was knitted goods that formed the major element in the woollen manufacture of Richmond and its tributary area. The town acted as the market centre for the merchants. Many members of the Richmond Corporation in the seventeenth century were hosiers or draper-hosiers and the standard method of apprenticing the poor children seems to have been to place them with knitters. In the seventeenth century a major export trade for stockings grew up from Newcastle and Stockton-on-Tees, both to London by coaster and to the Netherlands. Though finally Kendal and Dent replaced Richmond in this trade, Defoe in 1724 noted that 'you see all the people, great and small, a knitting and at Richmond you have a market for woollen and yarn stockings'.

As might be expected in an area of stock farming, hides were an important product as well as wool, so that tanning and leather-making were another important Richmond industry. Fieldhouse and Jennings record evidence of tanners from 1550 onwards and Baines noted three in 1820. In 1713 half the freemen of the guilds were involved in some aspect of leather production as skinners, fellmongers, tanners, curriers, glovers, cordwainers, saddlers and bridle makers.[18]

Speight stressed that later toll-free markets such as that at Leyburn undercut that at Richmond and to some extent replaced it, and Baines added Masham, Bedale and Middleham to this list. After the Dissolution and as new patterns of land ownership evolved, it was inevitable that the relative importance of the various markets would change. Several water-mills existed in the nineteenth century and Speight points out that the paper mills had been the major employers of labour in Richmond, but that by 1897 competition had affected them and they employed only thirty men. Baines in 1820 gave a very varied list of occupations that were practised in Richmond, but he did not list a paper mill. He did, however, note four corn millers, two ironfounders, three maltsters, three ropemakers, three tanners, seven weavers and three woolcombers and worsted makers.[19] This range of activities reflects the joint influences of the dale and the plain in the economy of Richmond. As the population figures in table 3 show, the town lost ground relatively during the nineteenth century and this is some measure of the decline of lead mining and agriculture in the area together with its isolation from supplies of cheap coal.

However, though it may have lost ground relatively in terms of growth, its status remained high. In the late eighteenth century its theatre, recently restored, became famous. Its buildings were given a Georgian facade and the Dundas family gave it added social eclat. Clarkson in the nineteenth century could say of it: 'The demand for houses of a genteel description is now very great ... the society is good, chiefly composed of persons of independent fortune who ... enjoy all the advantages of a polished and agreable intercourse.'[20]

As fig. 23 shows, a system of fields was organised when the new town of Richmond was laid out, in order to provide the inhabitants with as much of their food as was possible. Freemen, for example, had four beast gates in Whitcliffe Pasture and Wood, whereas stallagers had only two beast gates. There were various timber rights and by the late seventeenth century only those who paid their share of fencing costs were allowed beast gates. The medieval fields, East, West and Gallow Fields, survived in modified form as pastoral rather than arable land until 1810 when the Enclosure Act of 1802 was finally carried out.[21]

Knaresborough, like Richmond, also evolved around its castle, in this case with royal connections (fig. 24). It too was the centre of a major Honour and King John and later Edward II both used it. It was splendidly sited on the high northern bluff of magnesian limestone that stands above the river Nidd. First mentioned in 1129–30, its keep was built in the period 1307–1312 and the politically unstable nature of the area was

Table 3: Population Changes, 1801-1901, in some towns of the Dales

	1801	1871	1901	1971
Barnoldswick	769	3,187	6,382	9,943
Harrogate	1,195	6,775	28,423	62,427
Hawes	1,223	1,843	1,586	1,067
Ilkley	426	2,511	7,455	21,849
Knaresborough	4,202	6,178	5,105	10,500 approx.
Masham	1,022	1,062	980	825
Otley	2,332	5,855	9,230	13,265
Richmond	2,861	4,443	3,837	7,245
Ripon	3,211	6,143	8,230	10,989
Sedbergh	1,639	1,983	2,432	2,741
Settle	1,136	2,163	2,302	2,171
Skipton	2,305	6,078	11,986	12,437

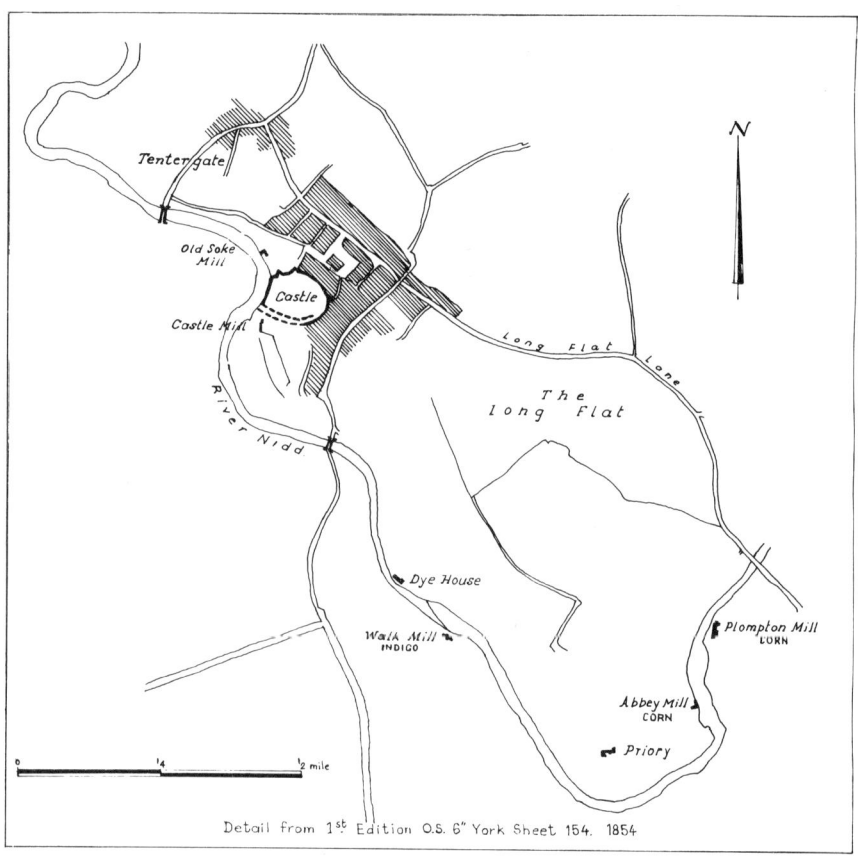

Fig. 24.   Knaresborough in 1854.

emphasised in 1318 when the Scots burnt the town but did not manage to
take the castle. The market is first mentioned in 1206 and the main
church, as in Richmond, is offset from the market place. New markets were
created by Edward I in 1304 at Hampsthwaite and Pannal and these
must have competed with that of Knaresborough.

An industry unique to Knaresborough in comparison with the other
towns described was that of iron making and forges were at work in the
area in the early thirteenth century. In 1227 forges were recorded at Pannal
and Haverah, using beds of ironstone in the Millstone Grits. The place
name Kirkby Overblow (Oreblowers) reflects its original importance as a
local smelting centre.[22]

The more typical cloth making activities also took place in Knaresborough and its surrounding parishes. A fulling mill worked in the town from 1284 and it was still functioning in the sixteenth century, but it was decayed by 1564.[23] In a very detailed and valuable analysis of the development of the linen industry in Knaresborough, Jennings suggests that the increased demand by yeomen families for house linen and the trade of lead from York and Hull to Scandinavia and Poland in the 1560s onwards, produced a return flow of cheap, high quality flax.[24] Jennings sums it up, 'the seventeenth century saw a series of changes which gradually transformed the local textile industry and eventually turned Knaresborough into a linen manufacturing town'. A particularly interesting local specialisation was that of dyeing and the Warner family were involved in this process; in 1646 John Warner was said to be undertaking 'much country work'.[25] The nature of Knaresborough as a centre of its area is stressed in this comment.

The first stages in the growth of what was to become Harrogate were to the advantage of Knaresborough. Until accommodation began to be built at Harrogate those who went to take the waters stayed at Knaresborough. In 1632, Michael Stanhope, who was singing the praises of the Tewit Well, had to admit that the Haregate-Head site lacked shelter and 'those that are weake . . . receive more prejudice by the piercing bleake aire, than benefit by the water'.[26] In 1642 the hope was expressed that a competent new Vicar of Knaresborough would be appointed as 'the towne stands in need of such a one in regard to the largeness of it and the great resort to it in summer time by reason of the wells'.[27]

In the eighteenth century the water-powered factory stage of linen-making meant that the linen industry became less concentrated in Knaresborough. Despite two attempts, no canal was ever constructed to link the town with either the north-eastern or West Riding coalfields and the railway did not arrive until that from York was opened in 1848. By this time the growth of Harrogate had altered the relative importance of the two centres: as the population table shows, the ancient borough was fast overhauled by the upstart spa.

Skipton, as fig. 25 shows, has like Richmond also evolved around its castle. Again like Richmond, its growth really stemmed from the granting of a major Fee to one family, in this case the Romille family in 1066 and then the Cliffords from 1309. Dawson quoted a valuation of the Manors conveyed to Robert de Clifford in 1311 which was used as a basis for a re-valuation of the Clifford properties in 1609. The following extracts give a picture of Skipton in 1311 and some measure of the changes by 1609:

'The Castle, the yard and court thereof, 2 Acre & di., valued at ijs., & is worth no more, ijs. Two Corne milles, then worth 13.6.8., now worth p.an'm . . . xxxl. The parke adioyning to the Castle, then valued at lxs., beside the feeding & keping of the deare, & now worth more then that allow'ce . . . xijl. The p'fitte of the weekely m'kett & two faiers ther in the yere, then valued at xvjl., xiijs., iiijd., and the same m'kett w'th fower faiers & ev'y fortnight a faier ther from easter till Xmas, is but now worth p. ann. . . . . xxiiijl.

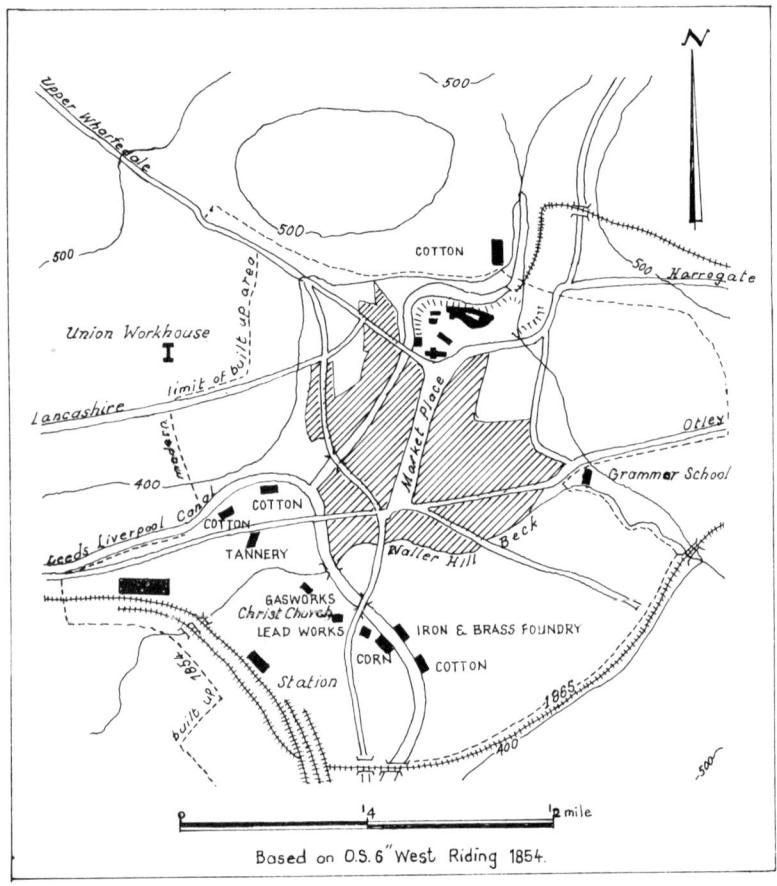

Fig. 25.   Skipton in 1854.

The lyster (dyer) fine or rent, then rated at xxs., & of long time hath bene decaied
& unpaied & now yeldeth but p. ann. . . . xs.
The p'fitt of te fulling mille ther when was xs. & now paieth butt . . . vjs.[28]

The market was well established by 1311 and King John had granted two
fairs in 1204. Dawson lists ten separate fairs from a return of 1756: three
Tuesdays fortnightly after Easter were for horned cattle and the Whitsun
fair was for linen cloth and mercery. The corn market was a special part
of the market in 1655 but by the 1820s this role had disappeared. It
was, and still is, as a stock market that Skipton flourished and flourishes.

As fig. 25 shows, the castle, on its well-protected site, dominated the market place and the fine parish church stands with it at the head of the market. The medieval town grew around the market place with its many inns, yards and craftsmens' workshops. Dawson gives an interesting list of the occupations in Skipton in the first half of the eighteenth century as extracted from the parish registers[29]:

apothecaries	curriers	ironmongers	shalloon-weavers
attorneys at law	colliers	joiners	saddlers
badgers (corndealers)	chapmen	labourers	slaters
bakers	farmers	millers	stocking-weavers
barbers	flax-dressers	masons	tanners
blacksmiths	flaxmen	mercers	tinkers
braziers	grocers	nailmakers	tailors
breeches-makers	graziers	plasterers	victuallers
butchers	hatters	ropers	weavers
carpenters	hawkers	soldiers	websters
chandlers	hecklers	sievers	
clockmakers	husbandmen	schoolmasters	
cordwainers	innkeepers	skinners	

This list gives a good idea of the range of activities in a typical eighteenth century market town. The wide variety of activities associated with servicing an agricultural area is noticeable. Like Richmond, Skipton shows considerable emphasis upon textiles and leather production: the shalloon-weavers, flax-dressers, weavers and websters suggest that it was clothmaking rather than knitting, however, that was the major textile activity.

Fig. 26.   Skipton Castle gateway.

SETTLEMENT PATTERNS

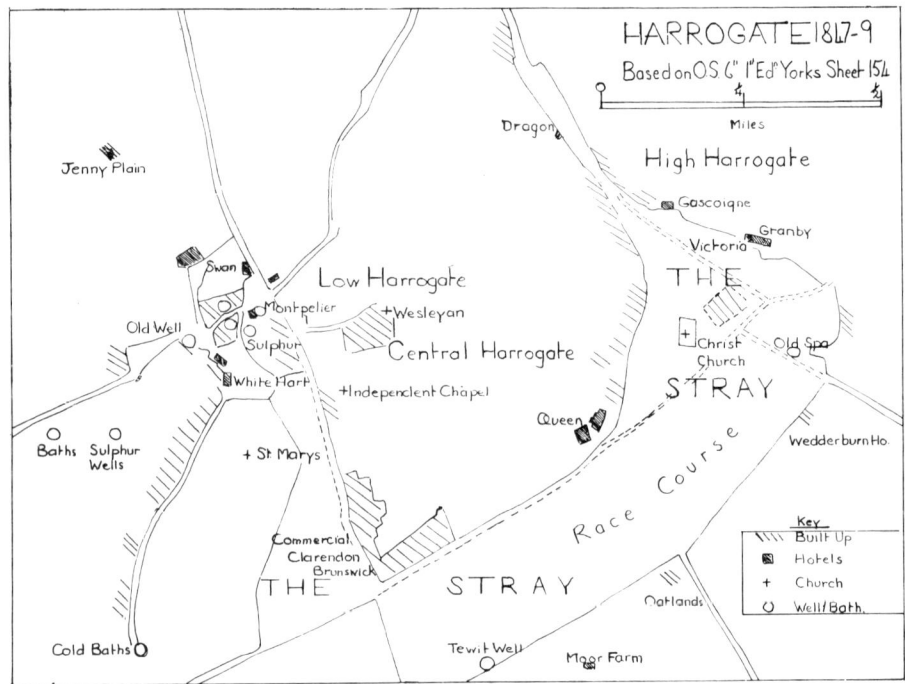

Fig. 27.

The arrival of the Leeds/Liverpool Canal in 1770 triggered off the industrial growth of Skipton and marks an interesting contrast with Richmond, where the swift flowing Swale proved too much for would-be canal builders. The quarries behind the castle were linked to the main canal in 1773 by the Springs Canal. A fulling mill and dye works had existed in the fourteenth century, but cotton manufacture got under way with the introduction of the first power looms into Skipton. A lead works was established in 1835; this reflects the supply of lead for the Grassington area. Paper-making, rope-making and corn milling were other local manufactures. The first edition of the Ordnance Survey six-inch map shows this canal stage of Skipton's industrial growth together with the first impact of the railway and the resultant spread of industry (fig. 25).

Skipton is now a very busy market and minor industrial centre: the Canal Head is being rebuilt and refurbished as a tourist attraction and its castle is probably in a much better state now than it has been since its earliest days. It is an attractive and interesting 'gateway to the Dales'.

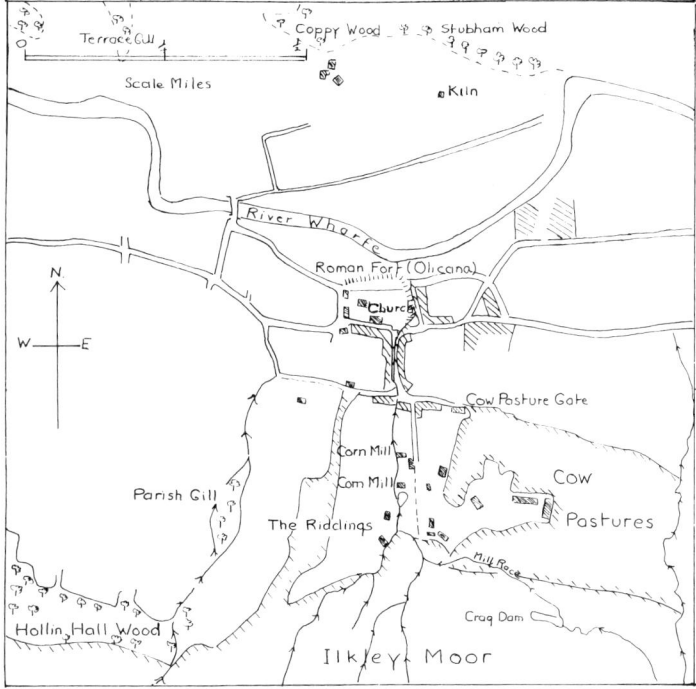

Fig. 28. Ilkley in 1854 (based on 1st edition O.S. 6″ sheets 169 and 186).

Harrogate and Ilkley had the fastest rates of population growth in the nineteenth century and both grew as spas (figs. 27 and 28 show how small both were in the 1850s). Harrogate did not exist as a separate parish until 1828 when High Harrogate was made a new parish—it formerly lay in the parishes of Knaresborough and Pannal; Ilkley was an ancient parish but it was a small village of only 426 people in 1801. A small anticline under Harrogate is responsible for the concentration of sulphur-rich and iron-rich (chalybeate) springs there which gave rise to the development of a spa.[30, 31] The White Wells spring at Ilkley seems to have no chemical peculiarities and it was the theory of hydrotherapy that led to the growth of Ilkley's major hydros rather than the actual taking of the waters.

Harrogate was already well known as a spa in 1697 when Celia Fiennes included it in her northern tour:

'Here in the compass of 2 miles is 4 very different springs of water: there is the Sulphur or Stincking spaw, not improperly term'd for the smell being so very strong and offensive that I could not force my nose near the Well, their are two Wells together with basons in them ... I dranke a quart in a morning for two days and hold them to be a good sort of Purge if you can hold your breath so as to drink them down ...'[32]

These distinctive qualities, perhaps surprisingly, became very popular and after the Civil War bath houses providing heated sulphur water baths began to appear. The first inn was the Queen's Head built in 1687. The new village of High Harrogate began to grow at the south end of the existing hamlet of Harrogate. John French wrote a booklet called *The Yorkshire Spaw* in 1652 and doctors, in particular George Neale of Leeds, began to sing the praises of the waters. A snowball process of growth then took place: as society took to the waters so more of society went, partly to meet the rest of it. By 1749 a new church, St. Johns, rebuilt in 1831 as Christ Church, was still in the parish of Knaresborough when it was built on the Common. The construction of turnpike roads did for Harrogate what canals and railways did for many other English towns, and the whole impetus for growth had been established long before the railways arrived.

The enclosure of the Forest of Knaresborough in 1770 had a very important condition woven into the Act: 'There are within the said Constableries of Bilton with Harrogate and Beckwith with Rossett ... certain wells or springs of medicinal waters commonly called Harrogate Spaws to which spaws during the summer season great numbers of persons constantly resort to receive the benefit of the said waters to the great advantage and enrolment of tradesmen, farmers and other persons in that neighbourhood, and the persons resorting to the said waters have always had the benefit of taking the air upon open parts of the said Forest'.[33] In acknowledgement of this valuable role the Act laid out 200 acres of land with free public access for those taking the waters: this became known as the Stray.

No major landowner undertook the development of the wells and baths and a complex story of the rise and fall of a variety of establishments followed. A firmer control on development came in 1841 when the Harrogate Improvement Commissions were established by Act of Parliament primarily to protect and improve the public wells.[34] This move led to the construction of the Royal Pump Room in 1842. The railways arrived from four directions between 1848–1851 but the central station was not opened until 1862. Visitor numbers rose fast. The first week of August in 1845 showed 1,515; by 1910 this had risen to 6,238 and Harrogate had become a key point in the national social scene, to be fitted in between the London season and the Scottish season.[35]

Whereas the market was a key element in the early growth of Richmond, Skipton, etc., it was a late-comer to Harrogate. It was not created until 1874 and its provision marked the progress of urbanisation that was completed when Harrogate became a Municipal Borough in 1884. The new borough gradually acquired many of the wells and baths: it bought the Stray in 1893 and by the beginning of the First World War its new big hotels and its hydropathic establishments as well as its spas drew 75,000 visitors a year. They were of the 'right sort' because Harrogate wanted to avoid 'the fashionable vulgarity' of Scarborough and it succeeded in maintaining its particular image until the Depression.[36] Since 1930 it has ceased to be a spa and has become gradually an administrative and conference centre with a wide range of government and business regional headquarters, so that it is now by far away the biggest of the group of towns in table 3.

Ilkley, as has been said, flourished as a hydrotherapy centre and the construction of Ben Rhydding Hydro in 1846, Wells House in 1856 and Craiglands, Troutbeck and Rock Wood House 'hydros' following the 1858 Parliamentary enclosure of the Cow Pastures common land all encouraged the rapid growth of the spa.[37] The railways from Leeds and Bradford arrived in 1865 and these encouraged businessmen, more especially from Bradford, to build their late Victorian highly individualistic houses in large gardens on a series of parallel roads laid out on the edge of the moor. The construction of a second bridge in 1904 led to a later growth on the north side of the river; this was also encouraged by the sale of the Middleton Estate at this time.

The response to these new pressures was an urbanisation of the former village shown in fig. 28 which had grown along the sides of a stream flowing north from the moor down the eastern edge of the ramparts of the Roman fort to join the river. Nonconformist churches were built in the 1860s and 1870s. The stream was covered, the new grammar school built and finally in 1892 the Ilkley Local Board bought the 'manorial' rights of the 'the moor' from the Lord of the Manor.[38] The area was created an Urban District by 1891 and between 1801 and 1901 its population had shot up from 426 to 7,455; a marked contrast to the townships at the top of Wharfedale where the decline of lead mining and farming led to Buckden, for example, having fewer people in 1901 than it had in 1801.

Ilkley is now primarily a residential centre for Leeds and Bradford and is firmly placed within the latter's sphere of influence as a part of the Metropolitan Borough of Bradford which was created in 1974.

References

A. Raistrick, *Buildings in the Yorkshire Dales*, Clapham, 1976, has much relevant detail.
[1] J. Walton, *Homesteads of the Yorkshire Dales*, Clapham, 1979.
[2] M. Barley, *The English Farmhouse and Cottage*, London 1961, p.233 (hereafter Barley).
[3] R. F. Taylor et al, 'Three Cruck Buildings in Lancashire and Cheshire', Trans. Hist. Soc. Lancs. and Chesh., Vol. III, 1965.
[4] Barley, p.117.
[5] T. D. Whittaker, *History of Richmondshire*, Vol. I, p.8.
[6] T. D. Whittaker, *History of Craven*, 3rd Edition, 1878, p.141.
[7] H. Thorpe, 'The Green Villages of County Durham', *I.B.G.*, 49, 1951.
[8] H. Speight, *Romantic Richmondshire*, 1897, Ch. XII.

[9] N. Pevsner, *Yorkshire—North Riding*, Penguin, 1966, p.65.

[10] K. Darwin, 'John Aislabie', *Y.A.J.*, 37, 1948–51, p.262–324.

[11] N. Pevsner, *Yorkshire—West Riding*, Penguin, 1967, p.228.

[12] Barley, p.243.

[13] B. Jennings, ed., *A History of Harrogate and Knaresborough*, Huddersfield, 1970, p.143 (hereafter Jennings H & K).

[14] Celia Fiennes, p.83.

[15] *Ripon: some aspects of its history*, Clapham, 1972, p.22.

[16] H. Speight, *Romantic Richmondshire*, 1897, Ch. II.

[17] as above, pp.74/5.

[18] R. Fieldhouse and B. Jennings, *A History of Richmond and Swaledale*, Phillimore 1978, Ch. 7, pp.177–187 (hereafter Fieldhouse and Jennings).

[19] E. Baines, *Yorkshire*, Vol. 2, pp.515–519.

[20] C. Clarkson, *The History of Richmond*, 1821.

[21] Fieldhouse & Jennings, pp.189–190.

[22] Jennings H & K, p.90.

[23] as above, p.93.

[24] as above, p.215.

[25] as above, p.210.

[26] as above, p.272.

[27] as above, p.223.

[28] W. H. Dawson, *History of Skipton*, London, 1882, p.11.

[29] as above, p.282.

[30] H. C. Versey, *Geology and Scenery of the Country around Leeds and Bradford*, 1948, p.26.

[31] P. F. Kendall and H. E. Wroot, *The Geology of Yorkshire*, Vol. II, fig. on p.852.

[32] Celia Fiennes, p.80.

[33] Jennings, H & K, p.235.

[34] as above, p.295.

[35] as above, p.311.

[36] as above, p.424.

[37] R. Collyer & J. H. Turner, *Ilkley Ancient and Modern*, Otley, 1885, p.252.

[38] H. Speight, *Upper Wharfedale*, London, 1900, p.220.

6
Farming in the Dales

Physical Controls

The absolute limits to the amount that land can produce are imposed by the physical environment. Wheat needs about 1,500 hours of sunlight for it to ripen: man may breed new varieties of cereal that will ripen a little more quickly than the older ones or will stand a little less rainfall but ultimately nature puts absolute controls on its growth. Similarly, stock have certain basic needs and the more specialised animals have become as a result of selective breeding so they are likely to be less tolerant of a wide range of conditions: our best meat sheep, for example, would not survive for long on the wet Pennine plateaux. The major controls imposed by the physical environment of the Dales are those of low temperatures and high rainfall. Professor Manley has pointed out in *Climate and the British Scene* that our mountains have a sub-arctic climate and that temperature falls surprisingly fast with height.[1] As cloud cover tends also to increase with height, so the mountains are less suitable areas on which to ripen crops or to carry all but the hardiest stock.

The mountains also give rise to much higher rainfall as well as having lower temperatures and this is a second factor that inhibits crop growth, directly because of lack of sunlight, indirectly because soils are heavily leached and therefore need an uneconomic amount of fertiliser added to them. It seems ironic to see lime being spread on fields that have limestone under them, yet a rainfall of eighty or ninety inches per annum can quickly leach out the lime from a soil. Broadly therefore, farming becomes more pastoral towards the high hills and more arable as the valleys open out eastwards to the Vale of York. Locally however, energetic farming, effective draining of land, careful use of fertilisers, etc., can mean that one farm may have more improved land at high levels than another.

The three air photographs (photos 54–56) illustrate the results of these controls on land use in the Dales very well. The view west into lower Wensleydale from over Masham shows a patchwork landscape with much improved land, yielding either cereals or hay. the More fertile soils of the margins of the Vale of York combine with the lower rainfall and higher sunshine of the eastern Dales to make cereal growing more practical. Stone walls have replaced hedges near Hawes in the second photograph

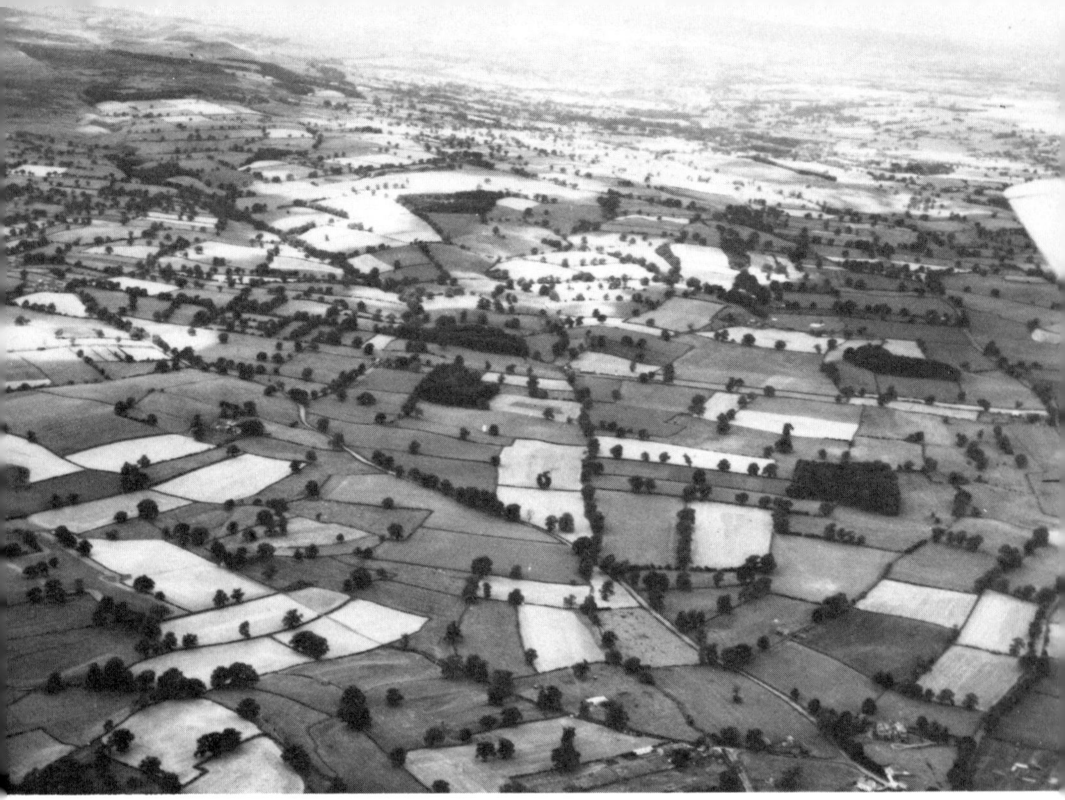

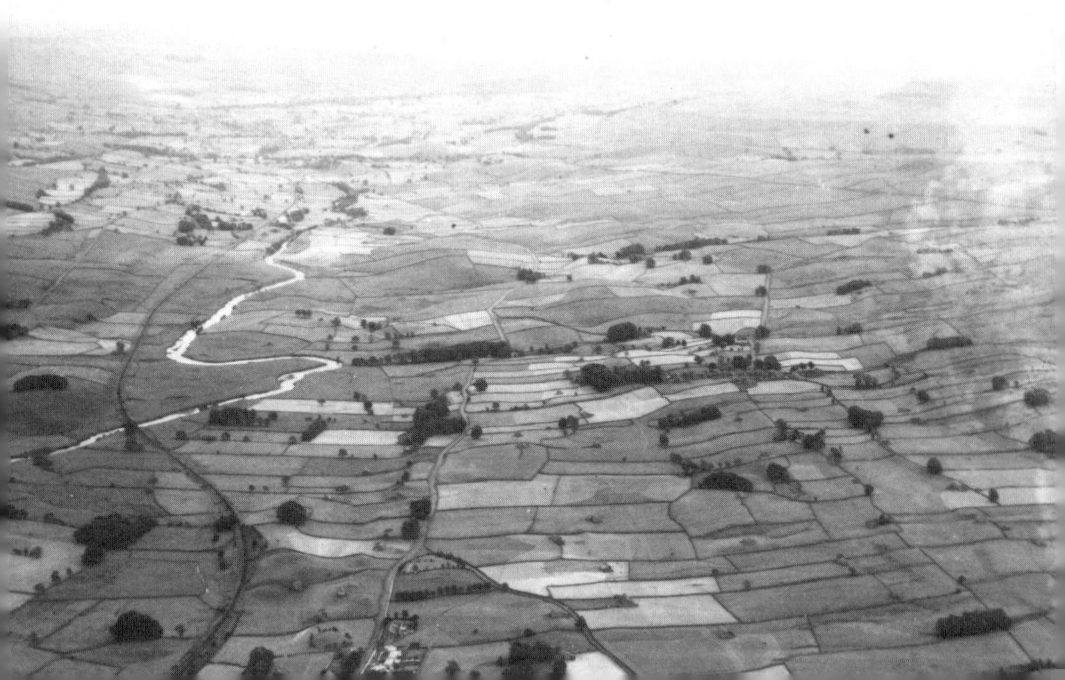

Farming patterns. **54.** Lower Wensleydale near Masham – hedges, former common fields enclosed in 17th and 18th centuries. **55.** Upper Wensleydale – stone walls. **56.** Pen-y-Ghent – high fell, rough grazings and 19th century enclosures. (Cambridge University Collection).

and there is much less cereal growing. Although the valley floor is still only at about 700 feet, the effect of the surrounding high hills is to give rise to much heavier rainfall than is experienced to the east. Animals are relatively much more important than crops. The third photograph, of Pen-y-Ghent from the south, includes much ground very similar to that in the sample parishes of Ingleton and Clapham and shows typical rough grazings of the higher falls.

The Pre-Enclosure System of Farming

As figure 29 shows, a township in the Dales had five sorts of land: meadows, pastures, rough grazing, an infield or infields and village enclosures. Three of these types of land were worked under rules common to the community: meadows were held in doles (individual strips); the rough

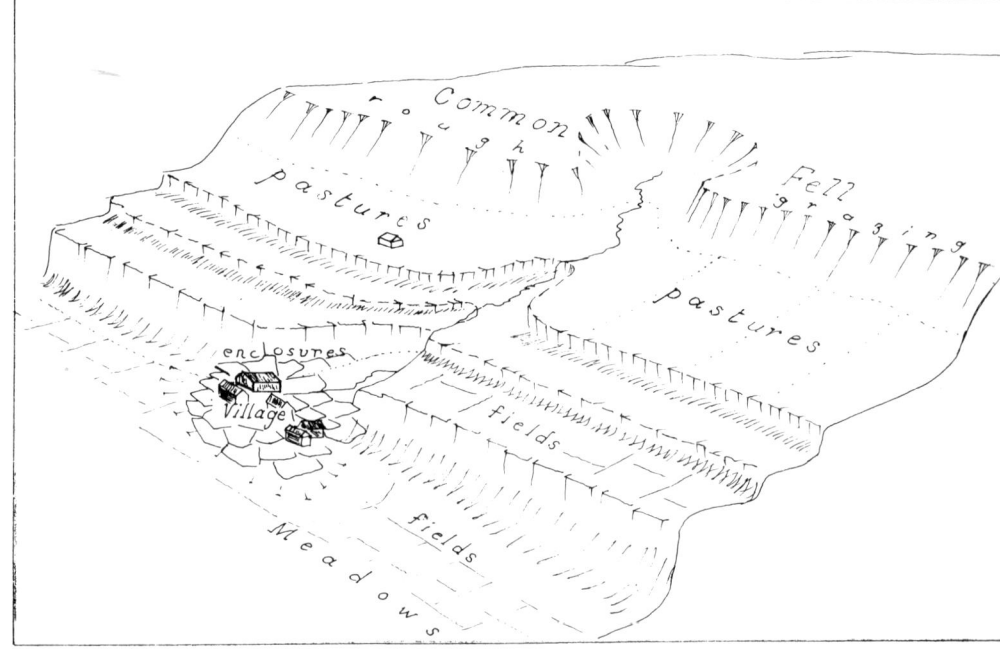

Fig. 29.   Land types in a Dales village.

grazings were very often 'stinted', that is subjected to rules limiting the number of stock running on them; and the arable infields were worked in individual strips under common rules. The pastures were more usually in private ownership and were enclosed by stone walls and hedges as were the small 'fields' around the garths or 'tofts'.

A glebe terrier for the vicarage of Thornton in Craven illustrates this layout of small enclosures near the farmhouse. After describing the house and its outbuildings it lists:

'two sun gardens adjoining to ye way to ye Hall doore, one fold on ye West end of ye house, one little court on ye North side, one kitchinge garden on ye North side of ye house, one little croft called ye orchard on ye North side of ye corne barne, one hay croft on ye North side of ye orchard garden. One field called ye Mastis ... one field called Kirkhill ... One meddow called Kirkeings wherein is one new barne where none was built before two years ago ... Four Kysbrigs which four buttinge on ye water called Crucible on ye north east end, and butting on ye way leading between Thornton and West Marton on ye South West side of ye Kysbrigs all which being enclosed.'[2]

Service tracks from the townships climbed up through the areas of small individually occupied fields away on to the higher hillsides and the rough grazing from which bracken was gathered in the autumn and peat cut in the spring and on which the stock were grazed in summer.

Grey, although not dealing with a single Yorkshire example, put the north and west of the county into Celtic Britain as far as field systems were concerned. He argued from Cumberland and Lancashire examples that the Pennine part of Yorkshire had single common fields (of a runrig type), or even perhaps originally many small individual enclosures that were in permanent use and other areas of waste that were only occasionally brought into cultivation.[3] The Carlton example quoted below, bears out this one field system as operating there at least.

A more recent survey of the evolution of field systems in Yorkshire by June Sheppard has some interesting suggestions as to the evolution of the arrangement of fields. The main emphasis in the article is on East Yorkshire but two ideas are of value. The first links back to Bishop's suggestion of movement of tenants from Pennine manors to the Plain of York after the Norman devastation. Sheppard sees this as a very likely period in which new field and village patterns might have developed: this would apply especially to the parishes on the eastern edge of the Dales region.[4] A second possibility, again more relevant to the eastern edge of our region, is that parishes that began on a Germanic pattern, with one big field sub-divided into long strips, may have expanded their arable land into the waste and reorganised the system to allow some fallow. A system of more than one field thus evolved from an original single field system.

Where a single field system was working it was in fine balance. If the population of a township increased, or if the infield was not carefully managed, difficulties could occur. Whitaker, writing of Carlton parish west of Skipton, illustrates this point.[5] In 1580 the tenants petitioned the Earl of Cumberland that because the town field was giving poor yields of corn, they might be allowed to sow the high summer pasture. The freeholders of Carlton objected that they had their own parts of this pasture, implying that it was only partly common pasture and therefore to create a common cornfield on it would pose difficulties. In all probability population pressure led to this issue arising in Carlton.

The lower parishes would have more complex field systems than those higher up the Dales. In 1549, Thomas Carr of Stackhouse, Settle, left his son '. . . a house in Settyll wt ye appurtances and other certain lands in Settyll Felds, Itm I geve unto my son Adam ye Grayn House wt ye lycence of ye Lord and other land in Settyl Feld . . .'[6] Here fields are recognised as opposed to the town field of Carlton and the mention of a grain house (granary) is interesting in view of the largely pastoral nature of the Settle area today.

The common rough grazings, the moors and open fells were spatially much more significant than the common fields, though the latter were much more important in terms of production per acre. We have seen in chapter three how important the great stretches of fell were to the

monastic herds of cattle and flocks of sheep. Many examples of the gradual
taking in of land from the common wastes can be cited. In comparison
with lowland Britain, townships did not press so heavily on the waste
because the number of the stock that could be kept was finally decided
by the amount of hay that could be cut in the meadows. However,
intakes did take place and at the end of the eighteenth century and the
beginning of the nineteenth, the high prices of corn and meat encouraged
landowners to enclose large areas of common in order to increase their
rentals. The general thinking of the 'Agricultural Revolution' also strongly
favoured enclosure both to increase production of crops and to encourage
farmers to improve their stock.

Agricultural Changes

(a) Parliamentary Enclosures

Whitaker was writing when enclosure was taking place on a large scale:
it would seem that his objection to the process was in the main an
aesthetic one:

'... yet enclosures, however convenient for occupation or conductive to improvement have
spoiled the face of the county as an object; the cornfields which by the variegated hues of
tillage relieved the uniformity of verdure about them are now no more: and the fine swelling
outlines of the pastures, formerly as extensive as large parks, and wanting little but the
accompaniment of deer to render them as beautiful, are now strapped over with large
bandages of stone, and present nothing to the eye but right lined and angular deformity.'[7]

Whitaker's home village was Threshfield and he was applying his remarks
particularly to the 'upper part of Wharfedale'. Here is a first hand account
of two very important changes that were taking place even before the
Parliamentary Acts of Enclosure began but were operating especially
strongly in the 1780s when Whitaker was at work.

The biggest single exercise in enclosure was that affecting the Forest of
Knaresborough. This huge area stretching 'from Clint in the North to
Swindon in the South and from Greenhow Hill to the Nidd at
Knaresborough'[8] was under forest law until 1770 when an Act of Parliament
was passed to enclose wide stretches of moor. The whole process was
completed by 1778 when the award was made. A new turnpike road was
made right across the area linking Knaresborough with Skipton. Stockdale
the surveyor who laid out the whole scheme, is quoted in Brown and
Shirreff as saying that despite the fact that most of his work was badly
executed, 'the forest, however, got in a great measure cultivated, and
rendered a wonderful increase of product to the public ... and though
scarce a single cart was before seen in the market of Skipton, not less
than 200 are weekly attendant on that market at present.'[9] The Forest of
Knaresborough was perhaps exceptional in that stretches of relatively low
moorland had remained as common. Further west and higher up the
Dales it was on the whole the higher slopes and the plateaux that had
remained unenclosed. Big acreages of these were also enclosed between

1770 and the mid-nineteenth century. Of the sample parishes quoted later in this chapter, Follifoot had 1,265 acres of common land enclosed in 1772 and Spofforth 500 acres in 1787. About 600 acres were enclosed at Clapham very much later in 1849. Of the other sample parishes, the Craven lowlands were already largely enclosed before Parliamentary enclosure got under way and in Swaledale, the Muker, Keld, Reeth and Grinton commons were enclosed in the early nineteenth century.

The effects of enclosure have already been mentioned within the ancient Forest of Knaresborough: in many other parishes also allotments, still often named as such on the Ordnance maps, are defined on the ground by straight stone walls which climbed high on to the fells. These may never have been sub-divided into fields but have been stinted to those gaining from the enclosure. In some townships, open fells, common to all in the township, were never enclosed, and it is these that remain as the 'true' commons (i.e. common to all freeholders of the township). Hoskins and Stamp in their study of *Common Lands in England and Wales* list thousands of acres of common land that were still surviving at the time of the survey by the Royal Commissioners in 1958.[10] Some of the areas of common fell are large and very important in terms of public access. They list Brant Fell (Howgill Fells) as having 11,000 acres of commons for Sedbergh, and Baugh Fell as providing 8,000 acres for Garsdale: in this latter case the sporting rights also belong to the freeholders of the parish.

(b) Tree planting

Whitaker praised Lord Ribblesdale at Gisburn Park for his great improvement of the Ribble valley. In the years after 1784 Lord Ribblesdale had planted 1,200,000 oak trees and many other species besides. Whitaker said: 'I know not a more patriotic work, or one which could better entitle its author to the barony of a valley so adorned and improved.'[11] When he reached Broughton in his account of Ribblesdale, he commented approvingly, 'the woods of oak, ash, beech and elm scattered over the whole estate, sometimes in large masses, sometimes in clumps and hedgerows, attest the wisdom and foresight of two former possessors, but of these species ash best rewards the Craven planter, while the oak is most ungrateful. A single ash lately felled near the house at Broughton was found to contain 500 feet of timber and sold for £45.'[12]

As has been said earlier, the planting of trees to 'improve' the landscape took place widely during the eighteenth century and the air photographs of Harewood and Fountains (photos 24, 47) show this well. The development of closes (modern fields) which replaced common arable and grazing lands also made the landscape much more wooded in appearance; the hedge timber was an integral part of the economy of the farms in the seventeenth and eighteenth centuries (photo 54). Rennie, Brown and Shirreff, more concerned with the practical than the ornamental, commented that on enclosure whilst land might not carry crops or stock 'it is our

57. Young stock in Grass Woods, Grassington.

opinion that larches and Scots firs would thrive in many situations. Wood of these kinds is much wanted'.[13]

However, as the air photograph of Pen-y-Ghent and the photographs in chapter one show, the Dales still have very little woodland. The National Park plans points out that only 0.5 per cent of the Dales Park is under broad-leaved woodland and that much of this is under threat, as is shown in photo 57. Some areas are now being planted with conifers, for example, Oughtershaw Moss at the head of Langstrothdale, and it will be interesting to see how these plantations develop. Of the 3,000 hectares (7,500 acres) of conifers in the Dales Park, 2,400 have been planted since 1966. It is estimated that perhaps another 10,500 hectares of land in the Park are 'potentially capable of afforestation'.[14]

There are strong arguments for this country producing much more of its own timber and for the work that afforestation brings with it. The aesthetic arguments are more subjective. With care it is probable that considerable areas of forest could be planted without spoiling the sweeping views and the general 'wildness' of the area.

(c) The Yorkshire Agricultural Society

The founding of the Yorkshire Agricultural Society in 1836 was another important step forward in the story of Yorkshire farming. Soon after its birth the society was offering a prize of £25 for the best Shorthorn bull, on condition that it remained in the county for nine months to serve sixty cows belonging to members of the society at not more than £1 per cow. A £20 prize was offered for a Leicester yearling ram on similar conditions. Leading landowners were strong supporters of the new society: the Earl of Harewood and Earl Fitzwilliam represented the West Riding as vice-presidents and the Duke of Leeds (Hornby Castle and Kiveton Park) and Lord Feversham the North Riding. At the second show there were prizes for fleeces from Leicester, Southdown, Cheviot and Moor sheep. None of the breeds for which the Dales are now famous—Swaledale, Dalesbred, Masham, Teeswater—is listed. This reflects the way in which specialised stock breeding has progressed in a hundred and forty years. Similarly, the Friesian breed of cattle does not appear in the early lists of cattle breeds. The evolution of the breeds of sheep and cattle to be seen in the Dales now, is dealt with later in this chapter, but the society through its annual show, now permanently located at Harrogate, and its annual journal was a very important disseminator of new ideas and techniques in agriculture that were especially relevant to farmers in the county.

The society awarded prizes for drainage schemes, for stony land farming systems, for improved permanent grass schemes, for road improvement and for the development of agricultural implements in 1836. All these prizes, small in cash value, must have done much to publicize the improvements which their award acknowledged.[15] [16]

Other societies were also encouraging general agricultural improvement and in 1784 the Society for the Encouragement of the Arts of Agriculture awarded its Gold Medal to William Dinsdale for his improvement of land on the moors between Hauxwall and Richmond by burning, liming, ploughing and crop rotation plus sheep.[17]

Agriculture in the Dales 1866-1974 — the statistical record

For the past hundred years, every farm has had to make annual returns to the Ministry of Agriculture. These are made available by parish and give us a broad idea of the ways in which the patterns of agriculture alter. The fullest account of farming changes in Yorkshire as a whole, can be found in Harwood Long's *Agricultural Survey of Yorkshire* where a great variety of statistics is given. Tables 4 and 5 are based on tables from this volume. In an attempt further to illustrate trends, the statistics from a dozen sample parishes, which are shown on fig. 31, have been selected (table 7).

The sample parishes were chosen in order to show the range of farming conditions within the Dales. Follifoot, the Ribstons, Spofforth and Stockeld lie on the west margin of the Vale of York and have always had much more arable land than the other parishes. Follifoot is now a parish marginal to Harrogate. Long Preston, Hellifield and Wigglesworth are parishes of the Craven lowland. Ingleton, Clapham and Austwick include some of the Craven lowland but are in the main parishes of the Ingleborough Massif, and Muker, Arkengarthdale and Reeth are parishes of the isolated dales par excellence. Clusters of parishes were chosen so that exceptional changes in any one parish were less likely to make the figures unrepresentative of the areas within which they lie.

The Government's collection of agricultural statistics by parish, began in

Table 4: Northern Pennine Dales: livestock per 1,000 acres crops and grass, 30 Parishes, 1962

(Selected data from Harwood Long, Table 34)

Cattle		No.	Sheep	No.
Cows in milk	—dairy	90	Ewes	1,905
	—beef	33	Ewes—2 tooth	465
Cows in calf	—dairy	50	Rams	54
	—beef	9	Draft and cast Ewes	42
Heifers in calf	—dairy	45	Wethers 1 year +	79
	—beef	12	Sheep and lambs, 1 year	2,100
Bulls		8	Total:	4,645
Stock 2 year +		30		
Stock 1–2 years +		98	Pigs	48
Under 1 year		131	Poultry	1,097
Total:		506		

Table 5: Number of Holdings in groups of selected Pennine Dale parishes, 1870, 1953 and 1962

(Source, Harwood Long, Table 30)

	Under 5 acres	5–20 acres	20–50 acres	50–100 acres	Over 100 acres	Total number of holdings
1870	356	578	406	254	219	1,813
1953	89	189	329	264	193	1,064
1962	69	127	238	284	201	919

Number of holdings in 12 West Riding Dales parishes, 1870, 1953 and 1962

1870	53	111	107	70	35	376
1953	32	72	85	70	36	295
1962	27	46	55	75	44	247

Table 6: Craven Farms (June 4th, 1962)

	Lowland	Upland
Mean farm size (acres)	177	397
Arable and grass	99	110
Rough grazing	77	286
Total farms in sample	224	139
Crops as % of total area		
Arable	nil	nil
Temporary grass	2·0	1·4
Permanent grass	54	26
Rough grazing	44	72
Stock per 100 acres		
Cows and heifers in milk	6·9	2·8
Other cattle	22	15
Total cattle:	29	18
Ewes	63	64
Other sheep	73	66
Total sheep	136	130

Figures rounded and selected from Tables XI and XII, Beresford and Jones

1866 and this makes it possible to make comparisons about the state of agriculture over the latter part of the period of agricultural decline in the nineteenth century, the two world wars, the nadir of English agriculture in the 1930s and the more recent recovery (fig. 30). The national decline in arable land and the increase in rough grazing, both show up on the table; the land use survey calculations for the North Riding show very similar trends to those nationally. The arable acreages are insignificant for most of the parishes but Spofforth-with-Stockeld showed a drop from approximately 2,400 to 1,400 acres between 1866 and 1906 and nearly a doubling in its acreages of permanent grass in the same period. The form of the returns makes it impossible to compare the rough grazing acreages 1866–1906 in the higher parishes. The small acreages of cereals and fodder crops grown in the Craven lowlands in 1866 had disappeared completely by 1906.

The Dales became an area ever increasingly of grassland during the period 1866–1939 and the rough grazings crept down the hillsides. Many farms went out of cultivation during these decades, leaving their pattern of crumbling upland walls and buildings and allowing the rushes and bracken gradually to invade their formerly hard-won enclosures.

The trends in stock are not quite the same as those for the rest of the country. It has already been pointed out that the abbeys, though being

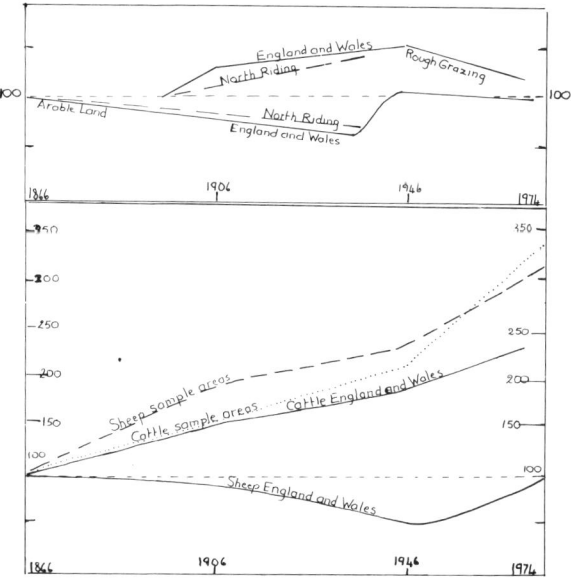

Fig. 30.   Agricultural change, 1866 - 1974.

Table 7: An Agricultural Summary: 12 parishes, 1866-1974

	Acres	Cattle/100 acres				Sheep/100 acres				Arable Area			
		1866	1906	1946	1974	1866	1906	1946	1974	1866	1906	1946	1974
Edge of Plain of York													
Follifoot	1,238	18	16	42	48	32	7	6	28	371	219	429	378
Ribston Great	1,912	9	21	25	27	60	36	22	53	634	683	818	1402
Ribston Little	844	21	28	26	13	43	70	?	?85	375	302	472	402
Spofforth with Stocked	5,344	14	19	29	43	25	42	36	97	1454 351	1239	1690	c2000
Ingleton Area													
Ingleton	17,858	7	10	14	20	39	85	105	146	—	nil	—	—
Clapham	14,720	4	10	14	21	14	63	96	120	9	1	233	nil
Austwick	5,400	14	24	26	37	43	100	91	150	4	nil	172	nil
Craven Lowland													
Hellifield	3,391	13	54	49	58	56	—	106	153	24	—	197	10
Long Preston	3,533	15	30	33	57	47	102	93	207	10	—	93	—
Wigglesworth	4,089	21	29	45	55	40	91	92	168	35	—	124	—
Swaledale													
Reeth	5,699	10	8	15	17	47	53	88	126	45	1	3	—
Muker	30,192	3	3	4	6	37	68	72	88	10	—	—	—
Arkengarthdale	14,566	3	3	5	8	43	66	94	105	30	—	—	25

Figures from the Annual Agricultural Returns, Census & Surveys Branch, Ministry of Agriculture, Fisheries & Food

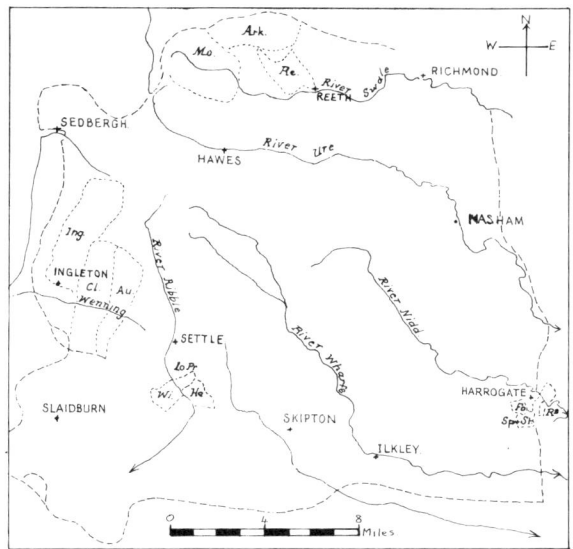

Fig. 31.   Location of sample parishes.

important sheep rearers also kept many cattle in the dales. But whereas the national sheep flock fell away sharply between 1866 and the late 1930s (the war was an exception) that of the Dales increased sharply. This national decline stemmed from the big reduction that was made in the flocks on lowland arable farms as a cereal, roots and sheep economy gave way to a more purely pastoral one. The density of sheep stock fell and the cattle numbers rose. On the hills, however, actual numbers of sheep and cattle increased.

The Dales have become an increasingly specialised stock raising area and have reduced their attempt to provide themselves with cereals and even root crops.

Farming now

The photographs (photos 58–61) show the main elements in the farming of the region. The first, taken in Upper Wharfedale looking to Buckden from near Cray, shows the meadows by the river with the barns (laithes) in which some stock may winter and over which hay can be stored. The steep, limestone sides above the valley floor are scree covered and wooded, and these give way to improved pastures which lie on the lip above the valley trough, probably in limestones. Finally, Scales Moor with rough grazings for sheep on the high fell rises above this lip.

An increasing demand for beef has also been an important factor to encourage cattle rearing in the Dales. The rich grasslands of Craven, both in the limestones and on the Craven lowlands, turned increasingly to beef cattle as demand for meat increased in the industrial West Riding. Dry dairy cattle were also sent to summer on the limestone grasses and return to the farm 'thatched with beef, full of hair and with a rare bloom',[18] ready to calve in the autumn. Table 7 shows the greater significance of the beef cattle on the higher Craven pastures.

The moors and upper pastures are still stinted. Cattle 'gaits' (or rights) can be bought and sold separate from the land, which is common either to a group of farmers or to a township. Stints on the moorland are more often expressed in terms of sheep: in Swaledale a stint equals 4 geld ewes or three sheep of any description. The number of stints held by a farm depends on the value of its enclosed land. Some commons such as that for Muker at Kisdon in Swaledale have summer rights for cattle and winter rights for sheep.

The aim of the Dales farmer is primarily to produce young cattle and sheep for sale and then to sell off the cows after they have had three or four young. The major markets to which the stock are taken are Leyburn, Darlington, Barnard Castle and Hawes in the north, and Skipton, Otley, Hellifield and Gisburn in the Craven area.

As table 5 shows, there has been a steady increase in the size of Dales farms in the last hundred years. The major change has been the sharp drop in the number of very small holdings: this was greater in the old North Riding parishes than in those in the old West Riding. A major factor contributing to this fall was the decline of lead mining: many of the two-income small holdings lost the mining part of their income and so the holding as a whole became more uneconomic. The economies of scale have also been operating: indeed Government help has existed to encourage the amalgamation of small units. This shows especially in the decline of the units of between 20 to 50 acres well after lead mining had ceased.

Long estimated that Dales farms produce about £23 an acre (in 1962).[19]

Of this income he estimated a half came from dairy produce, just over a quarter from sheep and wool and just under a quarter from cattle. This of course means that in total, cattle are much more important than sheep to the area as a whole. The 'average' size of dairy herds totals about twenty milking cows, but about a further forty cattle per farm emphasises the importance of stock rearing for sale. These figures (1962) emphasise

Farming in the Dales. **58.** Wharfedale above Buckden. **59** (inset). Laithe near Scar House, Nidderdale. **60.** Sheep on rough grazing, Ribblehead. **61.** Cattle above Cam Gill Beck, Starbotton.

the great importance of the twenty milk cows in these units and the significance of the monthly milk cheque to Dales farms in that half the income is from these cows. The average sheep flock totals about two hundred breeding ewes. In the 1960s it was estimated that this gave an average 'profit' to Dales farms of about £1,000 per year. The scale of the profit reveals that Dales farming was certainly not a way to instant wealth. On the other hand, many of the Dales farmers are owner occupiers and this gives them an independence rather similar to that of the 'statesman' of the Lake District—an independence on which it is very difficult to put a price.

Sheep

Most of the landtypes shown on fig. 29 are still used much as they were in the sixteenth and seventeenth centuries. The farms now have land of their own on the meadows and in the infields and some of the high intakes may be in private ownership. The high fell is still usually common and only subject to the Lord of the Manor's control and that of those with common rights.

In the 1780s the quality of the stock in West Yorkshire was not highly regarded by the author of the *General View of the Agriculture of the West Riding*[20]:

'there are so many kinds of sheep both bred and fed and they have been so often crossed that it is not easy to describe them . . .'
'upon the waste commons . . . the kind of sheep bred are the most miserable that can be imagined.'

The quality of the sheep is now very different and few farmers have the other sidelines such as weaving or mining that those of 1790 had; indeed the major agricultural concern of many hill farmers is the breeding of sheep and the production of a wool clip each year. The basic unit of the farm is the flock of pedigree breeding ewes: a flock numbering probably some three or four hundred (photo 62). With care and good weather this may rise at lambing time to nearly three times this number and farmers and shepherds vie to achieve the highest lamb crop per ewe. The two main hill breeds of the region are the Swaledale and the Dalesbred. Both are black-faced, black-legged strains that have been bred out of the earlier black moorland strain which the Scots evolved as the Scottish Blackface in the Southern Uplands in the eighteenth century. As noted earlier, moorland sheep were shown at the Yorkshire shows in the 1830s. Groups of farmers have gradually bred out distinctive subsidiary breeds

Sheep in the Dales. **62.** A Swaledale flock of ewes just before lambing time. **63.** Dalesbred ewes and lambs heading for the moors above Pateley Bridge (Edward Hart). **64.** Mule ewe lambs, sister sheep of the Masham, in Wensleydale (Edward Hart).

from this common strain and the Swaledale (photo 62) was the first. Becoming a recognised breed in the early twentieth century, it is now firmly established over much of the area as the basic breeding strain. The head of a Swaledale sheep with its distinctive white nose has been chosen as the symbol of the Yorkshire Dales National Park. The flock book of the Swaledale Sheep Breeders' Association describes it as 'a bold hardy sheep, well fitted to endure the hardships of exposed high lying situations . . . as mutton producers [they are] second to none.'

The Dalesbred (photo 63) is a particular strain of the Swaledale type that was founded in 1930 by the establishment of the Dalesbred Sheep Breeders' Association. The distinctive characteristic is the clear white spot on either side of the nose. The focal area of this breed was in Upper Wharfedale but careful breeding has led to the fleece being made free from any black wool and to its giving 4–6 lbs. of wool—ideal for carpets and Scottish tweed making—and so its price has risen steadily and therefore its popularity as a breed. Both these blackface varieties provide excellent ewes after three or four years in the hills for crossing with lowland breeds such as Leicesters or Southdowns to give Mashams (halfbred lambs) for fattening. Ram lambs (tups) and any surplus ewe lambs are sold off for meat in their first or perhaps their second autumn. The main Dalesbred markets are at Bentham and Hellifield.

Sheep farmers may be specialised breeders and if their farms have a great deal of hill land they may be primarily dependent on their sheep. However, as young stock can graze over grass and still leave feed for sheep they are often kept as well.[21]

Cattle

We probably see more cattle in the Dales now than have ever been carried there. Photo 61 shows mixed cattle high up on the pastures above Starbotton in Cam Gill, Wharfedale, at Easter. These are lime-rich slopes on the Yoredales: young Friesian stock can be seen from April onwards on any of the high limestone pastures around the Three Peaks. As beef prices rise, more farmers are finding the return on cattle becomes sufficient to encourage them to rear them. These pastures will never give enough grass for fattening cattle but as with sheep, so the farmers who breed cattle are supplying the vital young and hardy stock upon which the lowland breeders build their fattening flocks and herds. The records of the Yorkshire Show, as noted, reflect changes in the popularity of cattle almost as much as of sheep. The 'native' cattle of Yorkshire were a long horn breed probably not unlike the form that has survived to this day at Chillingham in Northumberland. In the eighteenth century breeders began to concentrate upon horn length and to select on colour and the white shorthorn bull became the most sought after beast. During the twentieth century the dairy shorthorn and beef shorthorn were bred out as distinct strains.

Sir Henry Vane Tempest was the initiator in 1812 of the idea of a shorthorn register: it finally appeared in 1822 and has continued ever since. Sir Henry's 'Buchan Hero', a Yorkshire Show prizewinner in 1841, was recorded as a Scotch Shorthorn type and his 'Dan O'Connell', a red and white bull, was the prize bull at the York Show of 1839.

Whilst many farmers will argue the milk and beef merits of the shorthorn their contribution to stock is still to be seen (photos 61, 65). After the founding of the British Friesian Society in 1904 this breed began to make headway and now many Dales farms will rear young Friesian stock because of their better potential as a milk breed.

The crossing of cattle breeds is as important as that of sheep. Another strain of cattle that has been very important in our uplands is that of the all black animal. The Galloway, a Scottish regional breed that can winter out and has a thick protective coat, is obviously well suited to the Pennines (photo 66). A commercially popular cross is that of the White Shorthorn bull with the Galloway cow to give a 'blue' or 'blueying' calf much sought after as a beef beast. Galloway and their crosses are often reared on the highest pastures suited to cattle.

Cattle farms are always searching for the strain that will give most meat or milk most cheaply and the 'mouse' coloured Charolais is now being cross bred on some hill farms because of its quick growth capacity. New strains such as the Simental have been brought in during the early 1970s in this constant search for the improvement of stock.

Dairying increases in importance as the valleys open out eastwards, partly because of the way in which the land improves but also because markets are nearer. The localised influence of the towns was perhaps more important before the days of the creation of the Milk Marketing Board in 1933.

In 1906 Rider Haggard, the novelist, made a tour of rural England. His journeys took him to Farnley Hall, Wharfedale, and Studley Royal near Fountains Abbey. The problems of those aiming at milk production then were well illustrated by his example of a tenant of Mr. Fawks of Farnley Hall who farmed at Stainburn in the Washburn valley. This tenant kept twenty cows and sent the milk to Leeds twice a day from a station four miles away. The family had to get up at 3.45 a.m. in order to do this, and half the cost of carriage on the milk had to be paid by the farmer.

Haggard was especially interested in the premises of the Skelldale Co-operative Dairy Society on the Marquis of Ripon's estate at Fountains. Butter and cheese of a 'Wensleydale character' were being made by the firm and Haggard was convinced that this local market was a factor in greater farming prosperity on this estate than on some others.[23]

Changes in dairy farming gradually took place as transport improved and patterns of demand changed. A farmer at Follifoot discovered that rather than make butter it paid him better to sell his milk in Harrogate.

65. Tough and hairy Galloway bullocks
(Edward Hart). **66.** New buildings in a
National Park reflecting an increase in beef
stock.

Having won the 1925 Yorkshire Agricultural Society Clean Milk Competition and using the advice of Leeds University Department of Agriculture, he improved his feeding using silage, piped his water, established a T.T. herd and developed a milk retailing business in Harrogate. Price was not a problem in a relatively prosperous town.[24]

The development of the Milk Marketing Board after 1933, together with its system of milk collection by lorry, centralised dairies and the monthly pay cheques to the farmers, was perhaps the biggest single factor in encouraging farmers to have some dairy cattle as well as sheep and to spread commercial dairying back into the less accessible areas of the Dales.

References

[1] G. Manley, *Climate and the British Scene*, London 1952, Ch. 10.

[2] M. Beresford, 'Glebe Terriers and Open Fields', *Y.A.J.* 37, 1948, Appdx. I.

[3] H. L. Gray, *English Field Systems*, London 1915 (reprinted 1959), p.271.

[4] J. Sheppard, Ch. 4 in *Studies of Field Systems in the British Isles*.

[5] T. D. Whitaker, *History of Craven*, Parish of Carlton, 3rd Edition, 1878 (hereafter Whitaker's Craven).

[6] Whitaker's Craven, p.162.

[7] Whitaker's Craven, p.4.

[8] B. Jennings, *History of Nidderdale*, Huddersfield 1967, p.47.

[9] G. Rennie, R. Brown, G. Shirreff, *A General View of the Agriculture of the West Riding of Yorkshire*, London 1794, p.75 (hereafter Rennie et al.).

[10] W. G. Hoskins & L. D. Stamp, *Common Lands of England and Wales*, London 1963, pp.338–350.

[11] Whitaker's Craven, Gisburn Parish.

[12] Whitaker's Craven, Broughton Parish.

[13] Rennie et al., p.33.

[14] Initial National Park Plan, Yorkshire Dales National Park Committee, 1977, para. 5.12.

[15] K. Hudson, *Patriotism with Profit*, London 1972.

[16] J. Fairfax Blakeborough, 'The Centenary of the Yorkshire Agricultural Society', *Journal of the Yorkshire Agricultural Society*, 96, 1938, pp.99–110.

[17] J. Tuke, *General View of the Agriculture of the North Riding of Yorkshire*, 1794, p.119.

[18] R. Harwood Long, *A Survey of the Agriculture of Yorkshire*, Royal Agricultural Society of England, London 1969, p.52 (hereafter Long).

[19] Long, p.160.

[20] Rennie et al., p.31.

[21] W. H. Long & G. M. Davies, *Farm Life in a Yorkshire Dale*, Clapham 1948. A valuable and detailed study.

[22] Sinclair's *History of Shorthorn Cattle*.

[23] Rider Haggard, *Rural England*, London 1906, p.306–7.

[24] F. M. Huxtable, *Journal of the Yorkshire Agricultural Society*, 87, 1930, pp.99–108.

The following basic sources were used in construction of tables:

1 Annual Parish Returns.

2 *A Century of Agricultural Statistics Great Britain 1866–1966*, HMSO, 1968.

3 R. Harwood Long, *A Survey of the Agriculture of Yorkshire*, Royal Agricultural Society of England, 1969.

4 M. Beresford and G. R. J. Jones, Eds., *Leeds and its Region*, Leeds 1967, Ch. VI.

The major source on Yorkshire agriculture pre-1939 is the report of the *Land Survey: West Riding* by Beaver and a further report on the *North Riding*. These volumes were commentaries on the first Maps of Land Use produced by the Land Use Survey. Selected Land Use Sheets at $2\frac{1}{2}''$ Mile have also been produced by the New Land Use Survey, Ed. Alice Coleman.

7
Industry in the Dales

THE two major themes in the story of industry in the Dales have been those of lead mining and of woollen manufacture. A number of other minerals such as coal and small deposits such as Dent Marble have been locally important. Whilst wool has provided the major basis of a changing textile industry, flax and cotton have been locally significant as well.

Lead mining was concentrated in Arkengarthdale, the Greenhow/Pateley Bridge area and to the north-east of Grassington. The lead bearing mineral veins lie in the carboniferous limestone and in the Yoredale Series. The veins tend to follow the vertical joints and horizontal bedding planes within the bedrock. They are thought to have been formed in the Hercynian mountain building period (Permo/Triassic) (Table 1) when molten rock was intruded into the foundations of the Pennines: this cooled slowly at depth forming granite but in places the more liquid and gaseous material worked its way towards the surface along faults within the overlying Carboniferous rocks. The molten material with a low melting point melted the rocks on either side of the lines of weakness up which it came and this lime rich material crystallised as it cooled into calcium carbonate (calcite), barium sulphate (barytes) and calcium fluoride (fluorspar): in the core of these veins and then only occurring sporadically the lead sulphide (galena) was formed. The barytes and fluorspar both have modern uses but in earlier centuries it was for the lead alone that these veins were worked.

A vein (rake or lode) may run across country for several miles, for example, the Bycliffe Vein on Grassington Moor has been traced for three miles into Nidderdale at Ashfoldside. Within the vein the galena may have been patchy in occurrence as in the Cononley lead mine near Skipton. The earliest working of lead was on the surface where the vein outcropped. This was done either by digging out the vein, so forming a groove along the surface, or a little later by means of bell pits; these were shallow shafts with galleries running out from their base (photo 68). Shafts were gradually deepened, especially after the 1560s when the German miners who were brought into the Lake District to work the copper mines near Keswick introduced water wheels, pumps and improved furnaces. But their major technical development was that of driving

130

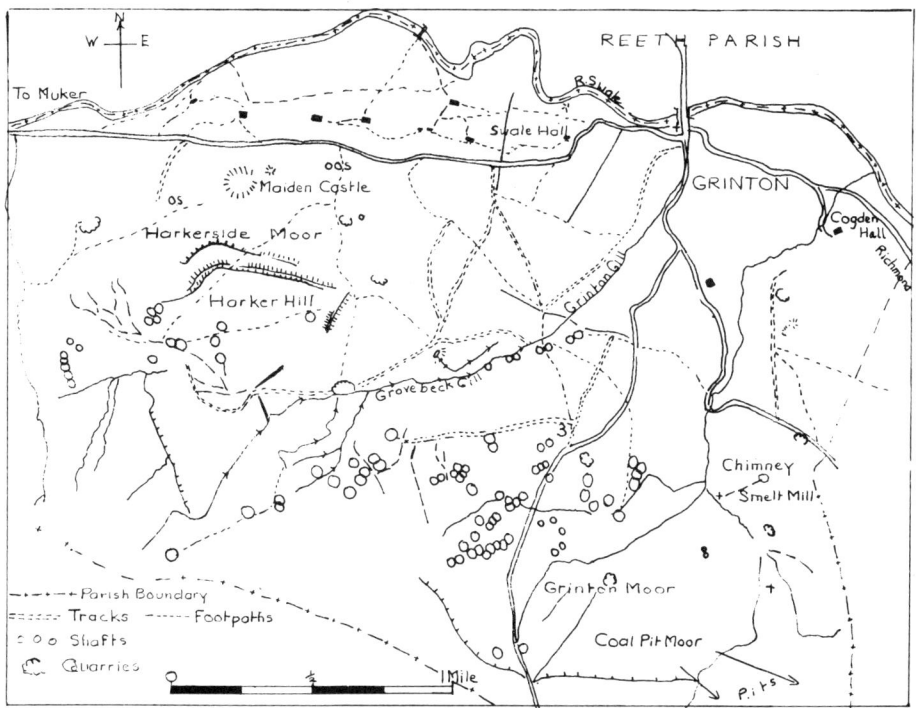

Fig. 32.   Lead mining and the landscape: Grinton in Swaledale (detail from O.S. 2½" sheet SE09).

horizontal levels low into the hillsides, thereby draining all the workings above the level.

The use of water wheels for driving lifting gear and for driving crushing hammers put stream sites at a premium, as did the improved methods of dressing (crushing) the ore before putting it into the furnace. Streams were diverted and dams built in order to provide a steady head of water. The Grinton Moor area in Swaledale, shown in fig. 32, has a number of diverted stream courses on it. The earliest use of water was for a very early form of mining called hushing: a flow of water was directed down a hillside where a vein existed in order to scour off the upper debris and to concentrate the ore at the base of the gully. There are several of these at the head of Grovebeck Gill on Grinton Moor shown in fig. 32. The last addition to the lead mining landscape of Grinton Moor came with the rebuilding of the smelt mill and of condensing as much of the lead from the fumes as possible so that they were less of a hazard to nearby plants and animals: the Yarnbury mine on Grassington Moor has a similar flue

Hebden Beck, Wharfedale – landscape of lead mining (opposite page). **67.** A restored mine entrance. **68.** Looking west to Yarnbury, with bell pits in foreground. **69.** Small fields – remnants of small farms held by miner farmers. **70** (this page, top). Miners' cottages at Greenhow. **71** (bottom left). A former lead mine in Trollers Ghyll, Appletreewick, still producing a little barytes. **72** (bottom right). Lime kiln at Conistone, Wharfedale.

system. The books on lead mining by Dickinson and Clough referred to in the reading list for this chapter give detailed accounts of many of the mines and also much detail on the actual processes of mining.[1] [2]

The working of lead has been an important factor in the development of the settlement pattern of the Dales and has thereby contributed to the landscape we now see (photos 67–71). Roman working for lead is proven by the existence of pigs or ingots of refined lead: three of these were found in the Greenhow area and one in Swaledale. The actual sites of Roman workings are difficult to establish with absolute certainty; Raistrick argues that as the Swaledale pig of lead was found at the Hurst lead mine it is likely that it began as a British mine and was taken over by the Romans.[3] The Elgees pointed out that Roman workings were to be seen on Greenhow Hill but gave no precise location.[4] One important aspect of the Roman search for lead was that it led to roads being constructed, for example, that from Ilkley via the Nidd valley near Killinghall to Aldborough which could tap the Greenhow lead relatively easily. The Cleckheaton-Elslack road passed very near to the Cononley mine and may have led to very early working there, though there is no archaeological evidence. The Swaledale lead was probably also brought to Aldborough and so to York, although it could also have gone across the moors to Brough and so to Carlisle. The movement of lead provides an early example of the system of links between the Dales and their surrounding lowlands which provide a constant theme through the centuries.

Little is known of any Saxon mining, but the Norman conquest triggered off a much greater interest in the deposits of lead. Castles such as that being built at Richmond by Count Alan and the new abbeys which were founded as the powerful new nobility endowed them with lands all began to use large quantities of lead for roofing and for water pipes.[5] Mines were also profitable possessions to the new landowners. By 1145 Count Alan of Richmond granted Jervaulx Abbey a charter to dig lead and iron throughout his Forest of Wensleydale. Mines were being worked again in Swaledale from the thirteenth century onwards. In 1279 Edward I granted John de Eston two acres of wood in his forest of Barden for the upkeep of the mill and the mine of Appletreewick.[6]

The improving technology of mining in England, dating from the introduction of German miners in the 1560s by Queen Elizabeth has been mentioned. In the days of small scale mining, each miner took his meer (claim) of 30 yards either side of a central pit on the vein. As mining became more complicated more capital was needed and groups of miners began to put up the capital for the sinking and draining of deeper workings.

The Dukes of Devonshire acquired the mineral rights of considerable portions of the Pennines: they had rights through much of the Peak District in Derbyshire near their Chatsworth estate but they also acquired

important estates in Wharfedale too. They retained mineral rights in the
Hebden and Grassington areas after having sold off much of their land.
In the later part of the eighteenth century the Duke spent £33,000 on a
new level that would drain the whole of the Hebden Moor area. A later
Duke built the Grassington Moor smelting plant. Mineral leases stipulated
that ore must be processed at this plant.

As mining developed in a community it initially provided alternative
income for small farmers, then it provided work for younger sons who
might otherwise have left home and finally if the industry really flourished
it attracted outsiders and the population of the community would begin
to grow. It is not easy to know what effect this industry had in earlier
centuries but in the eighteenth century many parishes began to record the
occupations of the father of a baptised child in their parish registers and
some assessment of the proportion of workers engaged in lead mining can
be made. The first mention of a miner in the Burnsall, Wharfedale, parish
register occurs in 1724. The Linton parish register showed a doubling of
baptisms between 1710 and 1740 as compared for example, with Ilkley
where the baptisms remained constant at twenty per decade during the
century.[26] This big increase in Linton's population reflects the growth in
lead mining on Grassington Moor as the fathers of many of the baptised

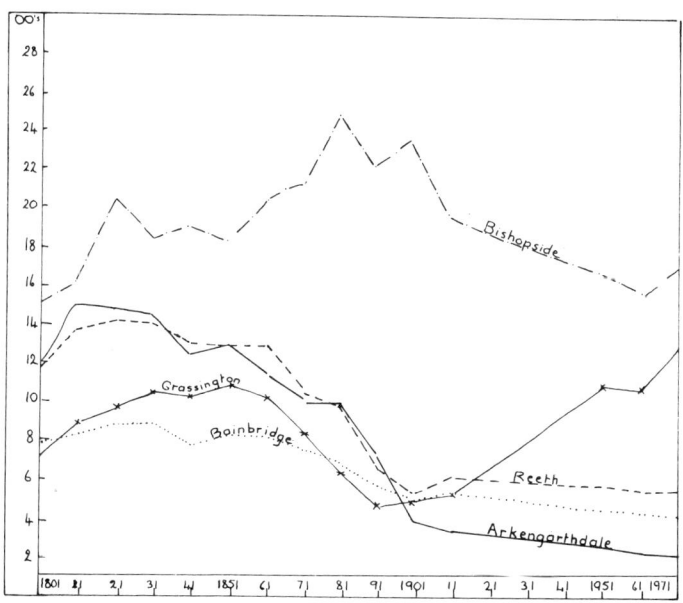

Fig. 33.   Population change in lead mining areas.

children were recorded as being lead miners; to a lesser extent it also
reflects the development of cotton spinning at Threshfield mills.

As the population increased, small farm units were established as part-
time farms. Photo 69 of the wall system at the head of Hebden Beck
shows such a pattern: the whole of the Pateley Bridge–Greenhow Hill
area has a scatter of now often derelict farmsteads and wall systems left
as the mining died out. Grassington and Pateley Bridge grew up as
important mining centres and little stone-built terraces, more typical of
industrial towns than of Dales villages, were constructed. The population
of these mining centres went on rising in the nineteenth century (see
fig. 33). Reeth, Arkengarthdale and Grassington show very similar trends
throughout the nineteenth century. As lead from Spain and South America
began to reach this country, the mines closed and the population fell.
This combined with and emphasised the general decline of population in
purely agricultural areas that went on in the period after 1861. The figures for
Bainbridge are very typical of the pattern of change of a purely agricultural
settlement.

Bishopside (including Pateley Bridge) shows a more complex graph with a
double peak. The census for Bishopside for 1911 has a footnote specifically
stating that depression in the stone trade (see below) and the closure of
lead mines were responsible for the decline of population. There was,
however, a lot of local employment in this period as Gouthwaite Reservoir
was built by Bradford Corporation. Scattered mining ventures have continued in the lead mining areas and some mines and waste heaps are still
being worked or reworked for fluorite and barytes. The detailed stories
of many of the old mines are being pieced together by the Northern
Mine Research Society. The fullest account of lead mining so far written
is that by Raistrick and Jennings, *A History of Lead Mining in the Pennines*.[7]

Whilst lead was the major economic mineral of the Dales, a number of
other minerals have been or are still being worked. In places coal has
been of local importance, though never in sufficient quantities to trigger off
the steam based industrial revolution that distinguished the industrial
West Riding from the Dales. The Dales coal is not in carboniferous Coal
Measures; it appears in thin seams within the Kinderscout Grits in the
Millstone Grit series and in one or two places within the Yoredale Shales
series.

There are some early references to coal workings: the canons of Bolton
were mining it in 1311, probably on Burnsall and Thorpe Moor. In 1334
the monks of Jervaulx were working it in Coverdale.[8] The Grinton map
(fig. 32) shows a number of coal pits on the highest part of the moor:
the geological accident of coal occuring so near to lead was very convenient
for a short period in the later nineteenth century when the steam engine
and improved furnaces increased mining efficiency before the price of
lead fell. A number of coal pits was worked on Garsdale Common about
two miles to the north of Cowgill tunnel on Mossdale Moor above

Garsdale.[9] Baines recorded two coal dealers in Garsdale in the 1820s. He also noted that coal miners accounted for a part of the prosperity of Reeth in Swaledale. Coal was only locally available, however, and its cost was even then a limiting factor on the growth of industry: Jennings notes that coal cost 8s. 6d. a ton at Skipton in the 1790s, but that it cost more than twice that amount by the time it reached the Greenhow mines.[10] Clearly the nearer a place was to a steady supply of cheap coal—cheapest near a mine, next near a canal and finally near to a railway—the greater its advantage for industrial development as the steam engine came into importance from 1750 onwards. It was this factor above all others that began to favour textile production in the Aire and Calder valleys from 1750 onwards.

Whilst the coal of the Dales was found in the Millstone Grits and the Yoredale Shales there is one small area where the true Coal Measures outcrop. The Coal Measures have long been stripped off the high Pennines by erosion, but on the downthrow of the Craven Fault at Ingleton, a small coalfield was preserved. A colliery was worked at Ingleton until the 1920s, just to the east of the town by the Skipton road. A number of small adits was worked on the sides of the Wenning and Greta valleys between Ingleton and the Benthams. The soft Coal Measure shales are easily undercut by the fast flowing streams and there are several stretches of surprisingly steep-sided valleys in this relatively low area. Within the Coal Measures at Burton in Lonsdale there are also clays that will kiln well and there has been a local pottery industry there; two potteries are marked on the 2½-inch O.S. sheet, one at Burton itself, by the river, and a second at Barnoldswick.

In upper Nidderdale coal seams lay above and below the Grassington Grit and the most important mine was worked at Woogill (Newhouse Edge) and Foggyshaw (Scarham Edge) on the south side of the valley. The first lease was recorded in 1791: in the 1860s a new level was driven to drain Woogill colliery and in 1869 the mine was working fully but its date of closure is not known.[11]

One of the most distinctive features of the Dales is that of the outcrops of stone on the hillsides which, because of their rythmic successions and horizontal bedding, give rise to the stepped nature of so many Dales valley sides and the tabular nature of many summits. Many of the more striking outcrops have become famous in themselves, for example, Malham Cove, Brimham Rocks, the Cow and Calf and Otley Chevin. It was inevitable, therefore, that man should make use of this plentiful raw material for his buildings and on Ingleborough is a classic early example of the way Iron Age (Celtic) man made use of the Millstone Grits to build the hill fort. Limestone, occurring in natural blocks, is less easily carved than are the sandstones so that door lintels, date-stones and window mullions are usually in gritstone or sandstone and it is these features that provide the major vernacular chateracteristics of Dales buildings, as can be

seen in the photographs of Bolton-by-Bowland church and Thorpe near Grassington (photos 73–5).

Quarrying therefore became an important activity after 1600. Quarries would initially provide for local needs but as transport improved those quarries near canal or railway began to have wider markets. The air photograph of Ilkley Moor (photo 85) shows the quarries near the Cow and Calf Rocks which were cut into the Millstone Grits. The rapid growth of Ilkley as a spa and the building of several large hydros stimulated the quarrying industry there. Collyer and Horsfall Turner wrote of the quarries at work on the moor edge in the 1880s and noted that the grits of Addingham Moorside were 'a fine-grained white sandstone, used for windows and door-sills and rough flags.'[12] Some of the hardest gritstones were used widely outside the area and Speight noted that the 'Rough Rock' was in demand in London as a foundation stone and had been used for the foundations of the Houses of Parliament.

In Nidderdale, quarries were also an important part of the nineteenth century economy. The biggest quarry was just up the valley from Pateley Bridge at Scot Gate Ash (fig. 34); it was linked to the railway at Pateley by an inclined tramway. Stone from this quarry was used for steps and platforms, for example, at the National Gallery. The blocks were noted 'as much as sixteen feet square without a crack or a flaw and are often raised entire of a thickness of only five or six inches.'[13] By the 1890s over 300 men were employed at Scot Gate. As other quarries were also operating, quarrying was a very important element in the economy of the Pateley Bridge area at the end of the century. Scot Gate Ash finally closed at the end of the First World War in 1918. Fig. 34 shows the extent to which a number of industries and quarrying in particular, were influencing the face of the countryside around Pateley Bridge in 1854.

A minor geological curiosity is that of the marble which was worked at one or two places in the Dales. Jennings suggests that the black 'marble' shafts of Fountains Abbey may have come from limestone at Blayshaw Gill. In Dentdale the famous Dent marble was worked on Rise Hill. This when polished to reveal masses of crinoid stems was widely used during the nineteenth century in north-west England for overmantels for fireplaces and for other ornamental work. Technically, these 'marbles' are polished limestones in which the fossil structures can still be recognised: a true marble is a metamorphosed limestone.

Stone in the Dales. **73** (top left). Barn doorway, Thorpe. **74** (top right). Bolton by Bowland church—west window and door of tower. **75** (bottom left). Farm building, Thorpe. **76** (bottom right). Mullions in Millstone Grit—The Manor House, Ilkley.

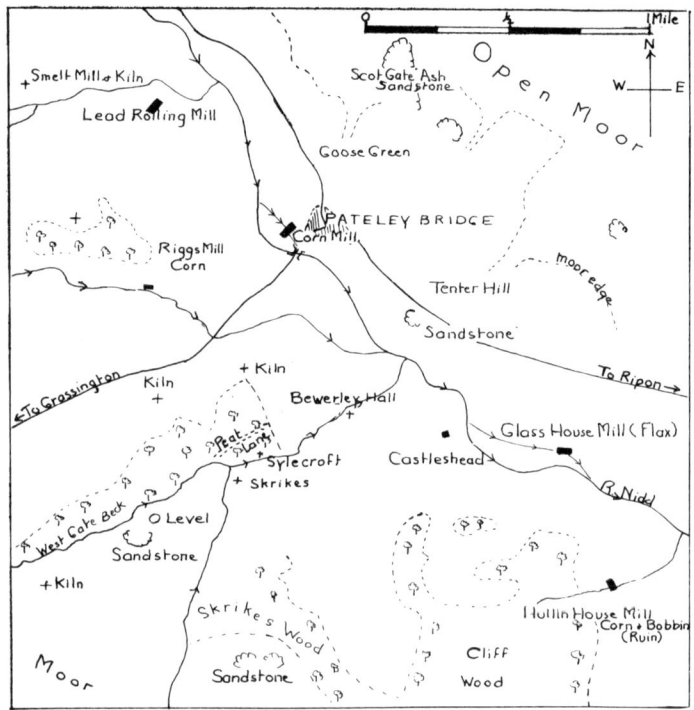

Fig. 34.   Industry and the landscape – Pateley Bridge (information
from 1st edition O.S. 6″ map, 1854).

Textiles
The rearing of sheep for the production of their wool has long been   an
important activity in the Dales. Yet the evidence is that the cow was
probably more important to the early settlers than was the sheep. The
chapter on agriculture discussed the origin of the Dales sheep and that
on the impact of the abbeys, illustrates some of their activities. It seems
that the abbeys began to introduce commercial flocks of sheep to produce
a surplus of wool for export to the Low Countries. Begging the question
of why it should happen there, there is no doubt that by the early thirteenth
century the Low Countries had become the centre of this very early
industrial revolution. Hull was exporting 1,000 sacks of wool annually
by the end of the century; most of this came from the Dales and then was
shipped down the Ouse to Hull[14]. About half the wool shipped from Boston
in Lincolnshire had come from the Dales.

This situation changed by the late fifteenth century; the number of cloths counted for tax collecting purposes had become the important item as opposed to raw wool and Yorkshire had nearly as many recorded as Suffolk. Lavenham in Suffolk recorded 1,000½ cloths in 1468/9 whereas York had 1,173, Ripon 693 and Halifax 746 for the period 1473/5. Ripon's figure is a reflection of a Dales cloth industry and that for York may also be to some extent: it was cloth and not raw wool that was the important product.[15] It is clear that Yorkshire was already an important cloth making district long before the industrial revolution proper got under way.

Cloth making was of course a domestic craft in the fifteenth century but it had at least one associated process which demanded the setting up of water mills. This was fulling the cloth, a process by which water powered hammers beat fullers earth (a naturally occurring Jurassic clay) into the cloth to consolidate it and smooth it. It had then to be washed again and stretched, on tenter frames, before it was ready for sale. One fulling mill must have served many weavers but it needed water power and this may have been a factor that assisted the movement of clothmaking further up into the Dales and away from the Plain of York. Early fulling mills were recorded at Ripon in 1184, Knaresborough in 1284 and another at Ripley in the early fourteenth century. Much later in 1806 Leeds clothiers were sending their cloth to the fulling mills at Arthington, Harewood and Poole on the river Wharfe, and Baines noted two fullers at Arthington in 1822. After this date the industry was becoming more and more concentrated in the coalfield area of the West Riding, but there were weavers, fullers and dyers in Leeds before 1300.[16]

As the cloth making became more organised, the major Dales cloth makers developed at Ripon, Halifax, Leeds and Wakefield. Leeds replaced York as the cloth centre for the Dales to its west, perhaps partly because

Table 8: Craven Area: cotton mills listed by Baines in his 'History of the Cotton Manufacture', 1835

| Towns | No. of mills | horse power | | total no. of people employed |
		steam	water	
Sedbergh	2	—	50	198
Ingleton	3	20	40	186
Grassington	3	—	27	130
Kettlewell	2	—	11	38
Skipton	6	90	61	605
Gargrave	4	6	54	149
Addingham	2	—	65	288
Haworth	2	—	32	65
Settle	5	30	47	333
Colne	11	149	136	1677
Barnoldswick	5	20	24	172

of water power and partly because the craft guilds were less restrictive than those of York and Beverley. The finishing of cloth was increasingly concentrated in Leeds and in 1711 a White Cloth Hall was built to replace the old open cloth market of Briggate. Defoe in 1724 described Leeds as having the largest cloth market in England and named the main cloths being sold as broadcloths, kerseys and shalloons.[17]

The invention of the multiple spinning machine by Crompton and the adaptation of this to water power led to the beginnings of factory manufacture of yarn after 1750: the mechanisation of weaving came later with Arkwright's water frame in 1771. Old corn mill and fulling mill sites became valuable as sites where new spinning and weaving mills could be built. By 1800 many a Dales village had a worsted mill or a cotton mill. Wharfedale in particular had textile mills at Kettlewell, Threshfield, Hartlington, Addingham, Burley and Otley. In Nidderdale, mills went through a whole sequence of stages. The manufacture of cotton yarn and cloth spread rapidly in Lancashire after 1750 and mills at Threshfield and Addingham had a period as cotton mills. As the machinery invented for cotton manufacture was adapted to woollen manufacture, it was used to make the light woollen cloths know as worsted. Wool was always locally available, but cotton had to be imported.

Flax and hemp were grown in the Dales, however, and fabrics could be made from both. The importing of cotton into Liverpool from 1700 onwards led to the development of the new lighter fabrics in Lancashire. Though some flax was combined with cotton initially to produce linsey wolsey and fustian, cotton soon replaced flax in Lancashire completely. However, in the Nidd and Washburn valleys, flax and hemp manufacture survived a good deal longer than they had in Lancashire.

Jennings in a study of sixteenth century Nidderdale inventories noted that of 143 household sheets listed, a half were described as being made of harden (hemp), less than a quarter of linen and just over a quarter of samoran (a mixture of linen and hemp).[18] During the seventeenth century one-loom woollen-weaver/farmers gave place to the two-loom linen-weaver smallholders who were primarily concerned with weaving linen cloth for the market. By 1744 a petition to the House of Commons noted 'that for eight to ten miles around Knaresborough they make coarse linens.'[19] In 1789, Hargrove, a historian of Knaresborough, noted that 'a considerable manufacture of linen has been carried on here for many ages and is at present in a flourishing condition'. Knaresborough at this date had an important linen market.[20] As weaving technology, through the invention of the flying shuttle by Kay, had moved ahead of that for spinning the demand for spun yarn outstripped supply. The incentive to install water-powered spindles existed and many old corn or fulling sites were converted to use as spinning mills or new mills were built (photo 77).

On Capelshaw Beck in Washburndale, for example, three mills were built—Patrick's, Little and Akers Mills. The sites of all three are now

77. Mill at Glasshouses near Pateley Bridge (see Fig. 34). Built in several stages from 1812 onwards and employing 264 workers in 1851.

under the waters of Thruscross Reservoir. It is estimated that more than £40,000 must have been invested in dams, watercourses and buildings in this small valley alone in the 1780s. The dams had to be large in order to store sufficient head of water on such a relatively small stream. Patrick's Mill was 300ft. long and four storeys high.[21] These three mills all ceased to work as flax mills in the 1837–44 depression; this suggests that this industry, though it was very important locally, was never more than marginally viable financially.

A longer lasting unit was that of New York Mills, three miles downstream from Pateley Bridge. This mill was owned by Francis Thorpe in the 1830s; he had made additions to it and the mill had three water wheels. Thorpe owned a main weaving mill in Knaresborough and used the New York mill for heckling (combing), spinning and cloth finishing: the finishing included bleaching, dyeing and calendering (rolling the cloth to tighten the weave and to impart a finish to it). Thorpe was still making linen thread in the 1830s and 1840s. He bought or built forty houses for his workers.[22] After 1825 a new church was built at Dacre Banks, a Wesleyan Chapel at Summerbridge and a Primitive Methodist Chapel at Low Laithe together with a Mechanics Institute.[23] The pattern of settlement and of social provision was changed in this part of Nidderdale as a result of this water-powered phase of the linen industry in the valley. Most of the mill buildings are now either in ruins or have a completely new function such as that of restaurants for example: in some cases the whole site of these mills is now under water. No fibres are now spun or cloth now woven in the Nidd and Washburn valleys.

Another offshoot of the textile industry in the Dales was that of hand-knitting. The knitting of both gloves and stockings became a commercial as opposed to a purely domestic activity during the eighteenth century. The demand for knee stockings created by the army during the Seven Years War (1756–63) established Dentdale's reputation and army agents toured the area in order to buy up large quantities of stockings.[24] Defoe, writing in the 1720s, noted that knitting had become an important activity in the Richmond area: 'here you see all the people, great and small a knitting: and at Richmond you have a market for woollen and yarn stockings which they make very coarse and ordinary, and they are sold accordingly; for the smallest sized stockings for children are here sold for eighteen pence per dozen or three halfpence a pair, sometimes less'.[25] The hand-knitting industry survived into the nineteenth century until the invention of steam-driven knitting machines finally enabled factories nearer the coalfields to undercut the isolated Dales.

References
[1] R. Clough, *The Lead Smelting Mills of the Yorkshire Dales*, Private.
[2] J. M. Dickinson, *Miners and T'Miners*, publ. author, 1972.
[3] A. Raistrick, *Mines and Miners of Swaledale*, Clapham 1955, p.19.
[4] E. & H. W. Elgee, *The Archaeology of Yorkshire*, 1933, p.135.
[5] A. Raistrick, *Mines and Miners of Swaledale*, Clapham 1955, p.20.
[6] A. Raistrick, *Lead Mining in the Mid Pennines*, Monographs on Mining History, Truro 1973, ch. IV.
[7] A. Raistrick and B. Jennings, *A History of Lead Mining in the Pennines*, 1965.
[8] P. F. Kendall & H. E. Wroot, *The Geology of Yorkshire*, I, Authors 1924, p.205.
[9] A. Raistrick, *Old Yorkshire Dales*, 1971, Fig. 8.
[10] B. Jennings, *A History of Nidderdale*, Huddersfield 1967 (hereafter Jennings), p.271.
[11] Jennings, p.315.
[12] R. Collyer and J. Horsfall Turner, *Ilkley Ancient and Modern*, Otley 1885, pxx.
[13] Jennings, p.321, quoting WG July 1884.
[14] H. C. Darby, *Histoical Geography of England*, Cambridge 1951, fig. 49.
[15] J. Mitchell, *Historical Geography*, Cambridge 1954, figs. 43 and 44.
[16] M. Beresford and G. R. J. Jones, *Leeds and its Region*, p.134.
[17] D. Defoe, *A Tour through the whole island of Great Britain*, Penguin Edition 1971, pp.500–502.
[18] Jennings, p.171.
[19] Jennings, p.177.
[20] Jennings, p.180, quoting Hargrave's *History of Knaresborough* 1789.
[21] Jennings, p.232.
[22] Jennings, p.239.
[23] Jennings, p.243.
[24] R. & L. Hinson, *Dentdale and Garsdale*, Dalesman 1951, p.10.
[25] Defoe, p.513.
[26] Parish Registers for these parishes reprinted by the Yorkshire Parish Register Society: Burnsall 1590–1900 (4 Vols.), Linton 1590–1812 (2 Vols.), Ilkley 1590–1812.

8
Communications

THE map of the relief and drainage of the Dales (fig. 1) has many features in common with that showing the main elements in the pattern of communication (fig. 35). Each of the valleys forms a natural routeway and the main cols between valleys were the obvious controls upon the routes linking them: Tan Hill, claimant to the title of the highest inn in England; Mallerstang, Birkdale Common and the head of Garsdale are good examples of places where natural routes are followed by constructed roads. The significance of some early controls on routeways has been mentioned already in the case of the Bronze Age route which followed Rombalds Way and the routes from the great abbeys such as Fountains to their granges and grazing grounds in the high fells to the west: these often cut across the grain of the main valleys.

Lead mining in Upper Wharfedale and in Arkengathdale was very important from Roman times onwards. Three Roman pigs of lead have been found and these discoveries suggest that certain lines of movement were followed; the system of Roman roads that served the area reflected the search for lead and also the need to establish a firm military control over the region.[1] The great Roman road (via) of the eastern edge of the region ran from Castleford to Tadcaster and on to Aldborough and Scotch Corner. There the routes diverged; the road to the north-west ran on to Greta Bridge, Brough, Appleby and then to Carlisle. This road defines the northern boundary to our region. The Aire Valley was not followed by a Roman road directly, but the fort at Elslack controlled the Aire Gap. The Roman road up the Lune Valley followed the western limits of the area (fig. 7).[2]

Within the region, Ilkley and Bainbridge were important forts: the lines of the roads to and from Bainbridge are far from clear. One or two other roads such as that from Elslack to Aldborough would seem to have been built to allow the exploitation of lead depositis such as those in the Greenhow Hill area.

The functions of post Norman roads were varied: the administrators had to move between the various manors of the great estates—those of the Archbishop of York for example. Cattle and sheep had to be taken to market in the autumn from the high pastures in the upper Dales so that roads leading to the market were important. Wide walled lanes were ideal for this purpose (photo 78); tracks for pack ponies could be much more direct than those for waggon carts. Weavers would carry their cloth to the markets in Ripon, Kendal or Halifax via such routes. Pack-horse bridges were built of stone at the more difficult crossing points of the fast-flowing streams (photo 79).

In the Forest of Knaresborough the system of compulsory labour on the roads for two days in the year began in 1528: the Highways Act of 1555 established that ordinary householders had to put in four days' work a year throughout England.[5] This Act made parishes or townships responsible for road maintenance. It probably reflected the increasing population of the kingdom and also the increasing trade taking place between the various regions. The Justices of the Peace had the authority to carry out repairs to a road and to charge a parish for its failure to keep its roads in a good state of repair.

Bridges were key points and their importance is reflected in that bequests were made in wills for their upkeep. In 1544 Maud Beckwith of Clint Hall left 13s. 4d. for the repair of Hampsthwaite bridge.[6] Daniel Defoe was struck by the bridges of the north, and when travelling north from Leeds he described his journey as follows: 'From the Wharfe we went directly north, over a continued waste of black, ill looking, desolate moors, over which travellers are guided, like race horses, by posts set up for fear of bogs and holes, to a town called Ripley that stands upon . . . the Nyd, smaller than the Wharfe, but furiously rapid, and very dangerous to pass in many places, especially upon sudden rains. Notwithstanding such lofty, high built bridges as are not to be seen over such small rivers in any other place . . .'[7]

It was not until the turnpikes were constructed in the latter half of the eighteenth century that the speed and comfort of road travel began to improve.[3] Few turnpikes were, however, built within the area of the Dales though a number went round its edges. Baines writing in 1823 records that Leeming Lane, north-east of Bedale, 'exhibits a fine specimen of the improvements made in public roads in modern times. This road is under the management of Mr. McAdam . . .' 'Blind Jack' Metcalf[8] had worked on the roads around Harrogate and Knaresborough and constructed the new surface for the Knaresborough to Boroughbridge turnpike in 1754; by 1777 the roads from Harrogate to Skipton and Leeds had also been turnpiked.[4] New surfaces and the better maintenance stemming from the existence of turnpike trusts combined to speed-up road travel. Coaches and waggons developed regular services to mesh with the improving system of water transport that was evolving at the same time.

Although the rivers of the Yorkshire Dales are very important features of the valleys they fall relatively quickly, their headstreams rising on the high plateaux. Whilst height in itself did not prevent the South Pennines being crossed by canals, the economic incentives to cross the Dales region

78 (above). Stone-walled stock road – Thwaite Lane from Clapham to Austwick. **79** (right). Packhorse bridge – Gayle Beck near Ribblehead. **80** (below). Track from Starbotton to Waldendale – gradient modified for stone and peat transport.

81. The Midland's Settle & Carlisle Railway. Looking south across Garsdale to Risehill tunnel. Dentdale beyond with Whernside and Ingleborough in the distance; Baugh Fell below. (Cambridge University Collection).

were never strong enough to lead to canal construction other than around the fringes of the region. Ripon (see fig. 22) was linked in 1767 by a canal to the river Ouse at Milby so providing an outlet for the corn being grown in lower Wensleydale and allowing coal to be brought up to it especially for use in the maltings. The *Tourist's Companion* of 1818 noted that coals and merchandise could come up the canal and that butter and lead, etc., left Ripon along it.[9]

The major canal of the region is the Leeds & Liverpool. Although it is very marginal to the south-west corner of the Dales its influence extended some distance away from the canal itself. Lord Thanet of Skipton Castle was a major supporter of the scheme for a canal to link Yorkshire coal and the port of Liverpool. The Act of Parliament was passed in 1770. The limestone behind Skipton Castle was worked for export and in 1786 the canal company leased these quarries; other quarries and lime kilns developed within easy access to the canal.[10] The section from Bingley to Skipton was opened in 1773 and Gurney Pearce was running packet boats from Gargrave to Leeds by the end of the year. Coal prices were halved in Skipton by the opening of the Bingley–Skipton stretch of the canal. The links on from Gargrave to Barrowford took much longer: the Foulridge tunnel was completed in 1796 but it was not until October 1816 that the whole route from Leeds to Liverpool was finally open. The Lancashire coal towns such as Blackburn and Burnley grew fast as did Shipley, Bingley and ·Keighley: Skipton may be seen as the outermost limit of the industrial region of the West Riding where the cotton and woollen districts met, but it grew much less fast as a result of the arrival of the canal than did Burnley, for example. Water supply was a very serious problem on the summit stretch of the canal at about 500 feet and reservoirs such as that at Foulbridge, built in 1795 and deepened at least twice, and that at White Moor, built as late as 1840, were needed to keep the highest stretches of the canal full. Whilst the canal is still in working order and may well have an important future as an amenity, it became less and less important as the railways began to replace it: the canal's best receipts were taken in the five years 1841–6.[11]

The Dales were initially bypassed by the main railway lines; as fig. 35 shows, the main London–Edinburgh line lay in the Plain of York, and the main west coast line, that from Lancashire to Carlisle which was completed in 1846, followed the Lancashire Plain and climbed to Shap summit. The Aire Gap, the natural route followed by a road, turnpike and canal, was selected for the North Western Railway (later to become part of the Midland). The first stretch of this line was built to link the West Riding with Scotland via Lancaster and to give the region an export outlet from Morecambe to Ireland. But in 1866 the Midland Railway company decided to put a line through direct to Carlisle and this led to the building of one of the most expensive and dramatic stretches of railway in England.[12] The line branched off at Settle and followed the Ribble valley; it involved the building of the Ribblehead and Dentdale viaducts and cutting of the Blea Moor tunnel, and then it ran down the Vale of Mallerstang to the Eden Valley (photo 81). By this time the main elements of the railway pattern were complete but several branch lines were later built in order to tap particular resources or to increase markets, especially for coal.

The need to link good coking coal from Durham with the non phosphoric iron ore of Furness led to the building of a line via the Stainmore Gap, Kirkby Stephen and Tebay. This was the South Durham and Lancashire

Union Railway, completed by 1862.[13] As with the Aire Gap, so this route which had been used by the Romans was followed in turn by the turnpike builders and the railmen. The relief of the land has exercised a continuous influence on the pattern of movement.

Smaller railway lines, often only single track, were constructed into the Dales. The Yorkshire Dales Railway from Skipton to Grassington was completed in 1902, as part of an otherwise abortive through route to Darlington and the north-east via Coverdale. In Nidderdale the case for the expansion of industry that would result from the construction of a railway was put by George Metcalfe Jones of Glasshouses Mill. A report published in 1820 had argued that coal prices would fall by a third, flax from 22s. to 14s. a ton and lead from 20s. to 1s 9d. a ton if a Nidd Valley line were built. By 1862 the line was opened and coal prices fell in the valley. A large crane was built at Pateley Bridge for loading stone: George Metcalfe proved the value of his own ideas and opened the stone quarry at Scot Gate Ash from which a tramway ran 1,000 yards to Pateley Bridge station.[14]

Other lines were built as alternatives and in some cases in competition with those already existing: the Leeds to Skipton line via Wharfedale was opened in two stages in 1865 and 1888 and its construction was an important factor in the growth of Ilkley as a spa.[15] Similarly, Harrogate was linked to Leeds in 1849 and to the main London to York line at Church Fenton in 1848,[16][17] thus ensuring the growth of the town as an important spa. It was not until 1878 that the line first built from Northallerton to Bedale and later on to Leyburn was finally completed by the North Eastern Railway to Hawes Junction, so linking with the Midland Railway. This was the one and only trans-Dales line to be completed and it came so late in the day that its impact was limited: perhaps quarrying and liquid milk production were the two most important industries to benefit from its construction.

Many of the lines which were built at such great economic and even human cost are now grassy trackways along much of their length: in Ilkley a car park occupies the space where a railway embankment once existed. The car and the lorry have revolutionised the transport of the Dales yet again.

Turnpike, canal and railway had localised but very important effects: we can view economic activities in the Dales as reflecting access to these three forms of transport. The whole economic and in turn much of the social pattern of many settlements sprang from their successive influences. The petrol and diesel engine, together with electrification, allow a much wider spread of activity. Farmers can take milk by tractor to a collecting point for the milk lorry, although even here bulk milk transport is changing things yet again. The small factory can plug in to the electric grid and lorries can carry goods anywhere in the county. The commuter can travel to his place of work from his restored cottage and, perhaps most striking of all, those who live in the big urban areas can easily have a day out negotiating the narrow lanes of the Dales roads in search of peace and quiet. Perhaps more of the Dales are now accessible to more people than ever before, though only a limited number actually wish to earn their living there.

References

[1] F. & H. W. Elgee, *The Archaeology of Yorkshire*, London 1932, p.135.

[2] I. D. Margery, *Roman Roads in Britain*, Vol. II, London 1957, Ch. 3.

[3] W. T. Jackman, *The Development of Transportation in Modern England*, Cambridge 1916, Cass 1962, Ch. II.

[4] W. Albert, *The Turnpike Road System in England 1663–1840*, Cambridge 1972.

[5] B. Jennings, *A History of Nidderdale*, Huddersfield 1967, p.182 (hereafter Jennings).

[6] Jennings, p.184.

[7] D. Defoe, *A Tour through the whole island of Great Britain*, Penguin Edition 1971, p.506.

[8] Jennings, p.183.

[9] *The Tourist's Companion*, Ripon 1818, Repr. Scolar Press 1972.

[10] W. H. Dawson, *History of Skipton*, London 1882, p.283.

[11] C. Hadfield and G. Biddle, *The Canals of North West England*. Vols. 1 and 2, Newton Abbot 1970, Chapters 3, 7 and 16.

[12] W. R. Mitchell and D. Joy, *Settle-Carlisle Railway*, Clapham 1966.

[13] J. Marshall, *Furness and the Industrial Revolution*, Barrow 1958, p.249.

[14] Jennings, pp.255 and 319.

[15] R. Collyer and J. H. Turner, *Ilkley Ancient and Modern*, Otley 1885, p.253.

[16] B. Jennings, *A History of Harrogate and Knaresborough*, Huddersfield 1970, Ch. XIII and p.306.

[17] W. Haythornwaite, *Harrogate Story*, Clapham 1954, pp.85–91, 107–108.

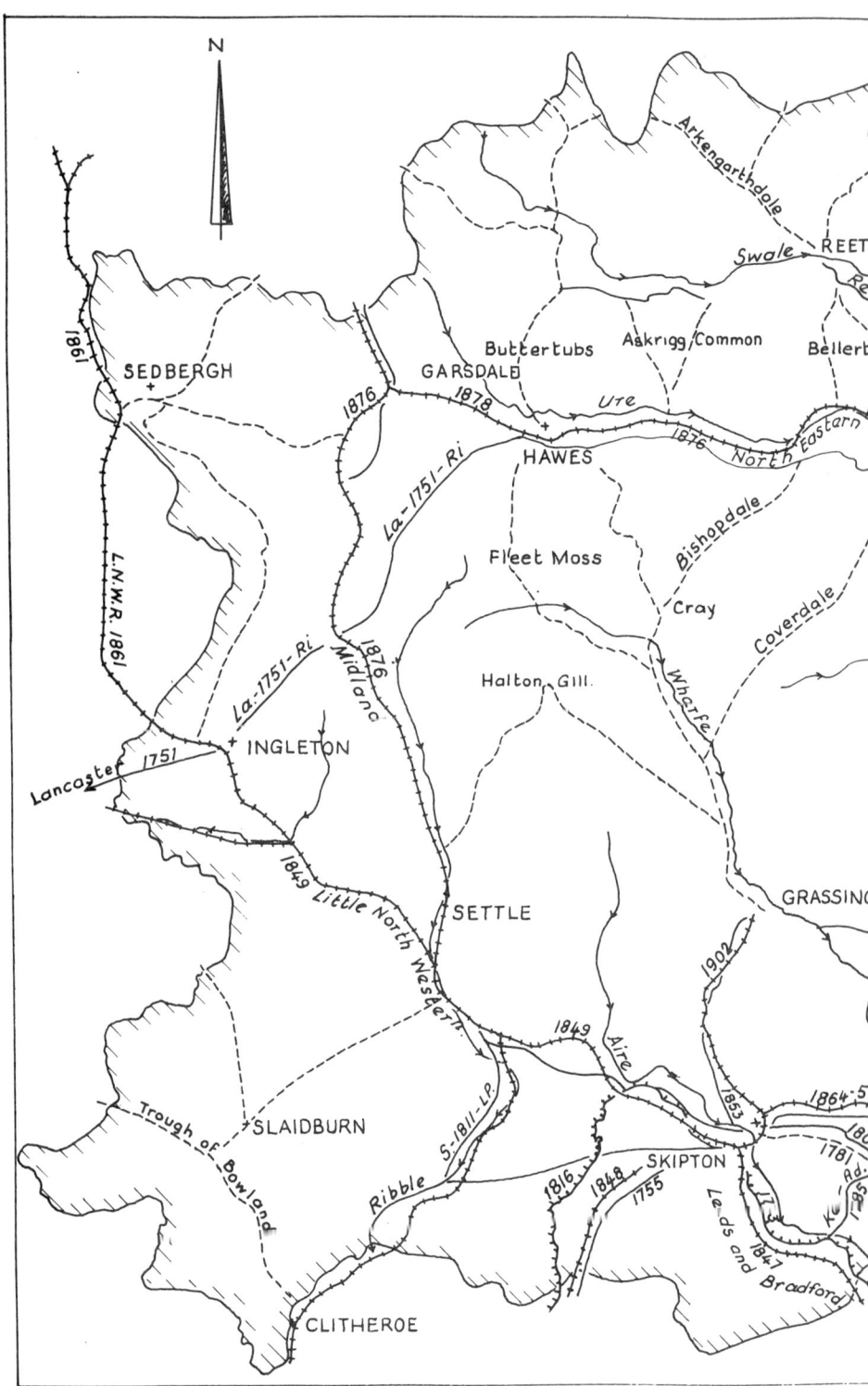

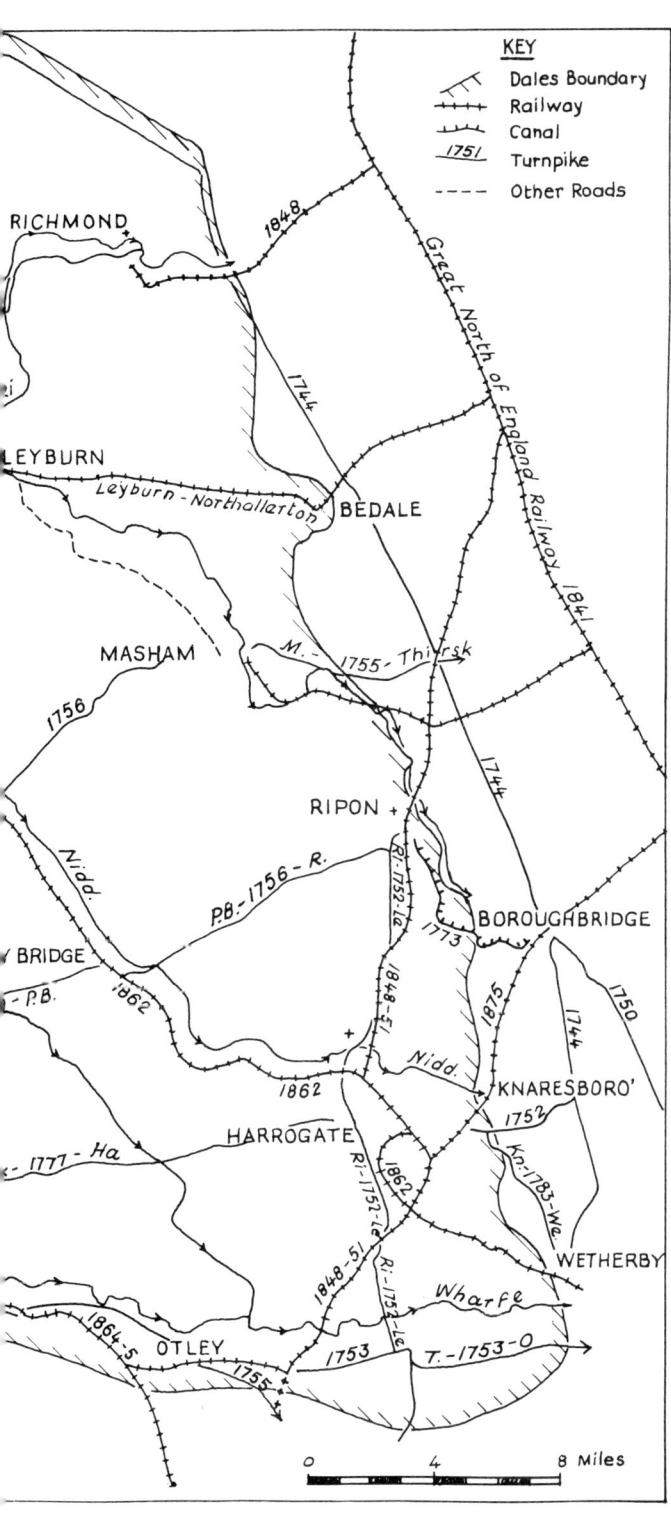

Fig. 35. Communications

9
Twentieth Century Issues

THERE are many forces shaping the face of the Dales in the later twentieth century. Changes are always taking place in response to new pressures at regional, national or even international levels. It has been shown that urban growth in the nineteenth century had two major effects on the Dales, it caused depopulation of isolated areas and population expansion near to the rapidly growing cities. National agricultural policies have repercussions on the pattern of the space-relationship between town and country. At world level the impact of the discovery of cheap lead upon mining in the Dales has already been discussed. World conditions of food supply, world oil prices and the policies of the European Common Market towards the more isolated regions of the member states are all now imposing new variables on top of the situation that existed in the mid-twentieth century.

Stock farming, water for human consumption, land for the urban population to relax in, land for timber production, important mineral sources, key sites of geological and botanical importance, unique buildings and many more claimants besides, all press for consideration in any discussion about the nature of the Dales in the last decades of this century. What is to happen if a farmer decides that he can secure a better living by letting his land out for caravans than by farming it? At what point should the nation step in and say no, the area must remain unspoilt? If the nation draws the line at such a point that the farmer claims it.makes his farm uneconomic will a landscape of derelict farms, used perhaps as weekend cottages, or of bracken-invaded pastures and of indiscriminate systems of footpaths result? Surely one of the great charms of the Dales is that a rural way of life can be seen to function in contrast to an urban existence. It is by seeing and feeling this rural pattern that many from the towns gain refreshment.

Central and Local Government and the Countryside in the Dales

Since the Second World War a new structure of local and national government has evolved which is concerned with attempting to seek a solution to the clash of interests that has been outlined above. Like everything that has been discussed, this system of planning has itself been modified and recently drastically reorganised. Much planning legislation has been enacted since the first Town and Country Planning Act was passed in 1947. All land and buildings not in agricultural use are now subject to the regulations imposed by the planning acts: for the first time in our history, building cannot take place at will. There are 600 listed buildings in the Park and these can not be demolished or altered without consent. The pattern of settlement from now on is one that is controlled by collective decisions as opposed to those of an individual landowner.

In 1954 the Yorkshire Dales National Park was designated. The North Riding County Council and the West Riding County Council established a Joint Advisory Committee and separate planning committees to administer the new National Park which was set up under the National Parks and Access to the Countryside Act of 1949. The West Riding County Council also had additional powers given to it by the creation of an Area of Outstanding Natural Beauty in the Forest of Bowland. Later legislation in 1967 further empowered planning authorities to designate Conservation Areas and Country Parks. At national level a number of key sites has been designated as being of outstanding geological significance or of great importance because of their distinctive flora and fauna. These are National Nature Reserves and Sites of Special Scientific Interest: within the Dales Park, National Nature Reserves have been set up at Scar Close and Colt Park Wood on the slopes of Ingleborough and at Ling Gill on Penyghent, all these being on the Carboniferous Limestones. Twenty- ur Sites of Special Scientific Interest have been designated within the National Park and the Yorkshire Naturalists' Trust manage another four nature reserves.

The Yorkshire Dales lie near to areas of high population density: whilst not under the extreme pressure of the Peak District, the Park must be the second most accessible 'open' area within England. Eight million people live within ninety minutes' travelling time by car from Skipton. All this means that the area can expect an increase in use: it might be argued that books such as this are over-encouraging the trend to use the Dales as a 'lung'. Increasing mobility means that the area will be subjected to ever-increasing pressures. The national motor vehicle forecast is that the total will almost double from 12 million units in 1971 to nearly 23 million by 1990.[1] This order of increase is obviously going to provide a major pressure on the Dales and raises the question as to whether a public transport system will have to replace the private car for those wishing to visit the area as opposed to those living there. Indeed the *Report of the National Park Policies Review Committee* (the Sandford Report) in 1974 stressed that 'the resources of park authorities, in money and skill, have from the early years of the parks been largely devoted to needs created by the motor borne visitor'.[2]

There is an increasing literature on recreation and leisure. The National Parks are now given a chapter to themselves in most geographical text books. The most important recent publications relevant to the Dales are

the Sandford Report and the *Yorkshire Dales Initial National Park Plan,*
1977. In these two publications the origins and philosophy of National
Parks and a critical review of their effectiveness to date are produced. In
the context of this book it is relevant therefore only to consider the
National Park as it is functioning and in particular to note its impact
on its area rather than to discuss National Parks in general.

As fig. 36 shows, the Park, with an area of 680 square miles, is about
one half of the total area with which this study is concerned. The boundary
of the Park is not entirely logical: it may seem odd that Nidderdale
and the Washburn valleys were omitted as well as Wensleydale down
valley from Redmire. The boundary skirts the Bolton estate in Wensleydale,
and Bradford and Leeds were opposed to their water supply zones being
in a National Park. The designation of the boundary of a National Park
did not depend solely upon the criterion of landscape quality. The county
boundary in 1954 was clearly an important factor in defining the northern
limit of the Park; it is ridiculous that Barbon Fell and the northern half
of the Howgill Fells should have been excluded, and similarly to exclude

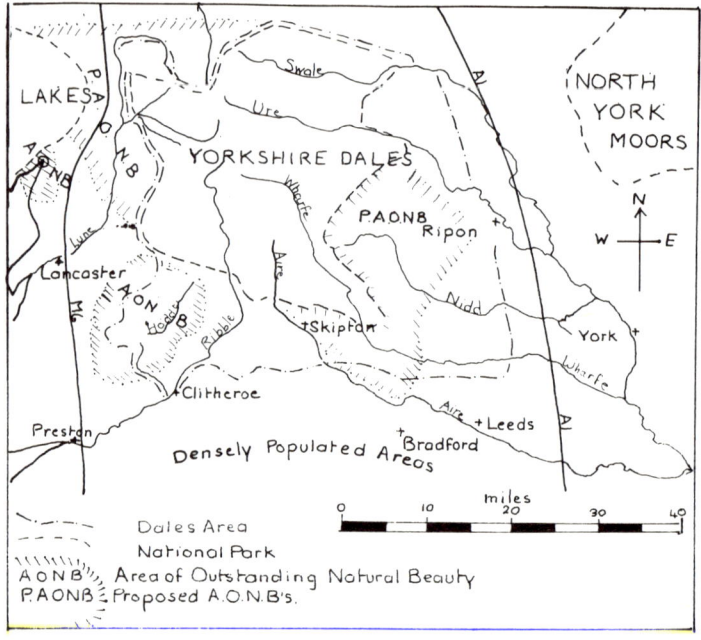

Fig. 36.   The Yorkshire Dales in their setting.

the moors to the north of Ilkley—Langbar—Denton—Askwith in Wharfedale seems equally illogical.

What does it mean to have an area categorised as being a National Park? The most important result of designation is that the Department of Environment via the Countryside Commission can grant-aid all work that is specific to the area being a Park with 75% of the total cost. The Park has no greater planning powers than any other planning authority but the General Development Order does not apply to Parks and Conservation Areas. This means that more control over building design and materials can be exercised than in less sensitive areas. It does not mean that any change in land ownership has taken place or that no development is allowed. Residential development is still taking place, as it must if settlement is to be able to adjust to new factors. New agricultural buildings are erected as in photo 65 and design awards have been gained for new farm buildings as at Burnsall Farm, Threshfield. Limestone quarries such as those near Grassington and in Ribblesdale continue to work (photo 87). Real clashes of interest would occur if very valuable minerals were discovered in economic quantities on the slopes of Ingleborough for example. Caravan and camping sites are strictly controlled; no doubt many more hill farmers would like to let out some of their land for these purposes if they were so allowed.

The committee responsible for administering the Park consists of 24 members, eight of whom are appointed by the Secretary of State for the Environment. This committee determines all planning applications within the Park. Since April 1974 the bulk of the Park and nearly the whole of the area with which this study is concerned has lain within North Yorkshire. Areas outside the National Park but within the Yorkshire Dales area have their planning applications dealt with by the relevant District Council planning committees. Under the Local Government Act of 1972 the North Yorkshire Councty Council, like all other planning authorities, had to prepare a Structure Plan by April 1977. This plan has now been approved by the Secretary of State. These plans deal with matters such as transportation and employment and form the basis for detailed planning for the near future. It is suggested that there should be until the end of this century 'provision of counter attractions for visitors outside the Parks, because these need to be dealt with on a regional or sub-regional basis as well as within the Parks themselves'.[3]

The Sandford Report stressed the need to bring people living in the Parks into the planning process: 'We believe it to be of first importance that imaginative efforts should be made to associate local people with the purposes of the Parks and to enlist their goodwill'.[4] This now happens and all parishes in the Park are consulted about any proposals for their area.

A new concept, that of National Heritage Areas, has been introduced by the Review Committee. In paragraph 3.8 they say 'because of the great concern we feel about growing pressures and demands on the Parks, and because of the deterioration on the quality of the environment we have observed in parts of them, some of us would like to see a new procedure introduced for identifying and protecting the area of the very highest quality of landscape in the existing National Parks and perhaps outside them. The first and supreme objective of policy for these relatively small areas would be to conserve their environmental qualities. Public enjoyment of a quiet and congruous nature would be a secondary purpose . . . such areas would be termed "national heritage areas". It might be interesting to play a game of listing the top candidates within the Dales for such National Heritage Areas! There will of course be many who will deplore yet another attempt to categorise and bureaucratise the landscape. In fact this concept seems to have received little support elsewhere and like so many past ideas it has been produced only to gather dust.

The hierachy of conservation is becoming steadily more complex and all this is to some extent rather sad, but if there were no system the pressures would almost certainly already have done far more damage to key sites such as Malham and Malham Cove or the Ingleton Glens than they have so far. It seems inevitable that some elements of public or private control have to exist if some very popular places are not to be devastated by the sheer weight of people.

The visible impact that the designation of the Dales National Park has had is limited: as it should be because the aim of its creation was to attempt to maintain the attractiveness of its landscape. Approach roads to the Park are marked at its boundary by the National Park sign of a Swaledale sheep. Photos 82–84 try to select some of the ways in which the Park has a visible aspect. Much progress has been made in the signposting of footpaths and in the provision of sensible footpath networks, as anyone walking in the Dales in the past ten years is well aware. Information centres are becoming more skilled in providing the right material for and in looking after many parties from schools and other groups who want a little more than just the ordinary guide books provide. The Dales Park has bought Whernside Cave and Fell Centre as an educational focus to encourage better understanding and enjoyment of the area. At some points such as Gordale Scar 'civilised' provision of steps is under way. Farmers receive about £4,000 per annum compensation for damage done to their walls. The warden service in its new style vehicles that have replaced Land-Rovers exists to try and ensure that people are shown how to look after the countryside. The voluntary principle is being encouraged and groups working on surviving features of interest such as a lime kiln at Kettlewell, are being helped by the Park in their conservation work. Is all this likely to increase public pressure on otherwise unspoilt areas? No land use planning issue ever has simple answers.

What will never be seen are the buildings, 'amenities' and 'improvements' that the Park committee and perhaps the Minister refused. Only by looking

82 (above). National Park warden service. 83 (below).
Malham car park, a National Park venture with information
centre. 84 (right). A footpath networks provides many
walkable routes compared with much of lowland Britain.

at back files of planning applications could one see what pressures there have been for change that were felt to be unsuitable. Planners have to stand by what they allow: they are rarely judged on what they did not allow or upon what is built as a result of their guidance as compared with what an applicant tried to build. The use, wherever possible, of local stone on new housing and new walls for road widening schemes is a major achievement by the Park in attempting to maintain the local character of the Dales. The Malham information centre on photo 83 is an example of this approach. New standards will become the accepted standards and in time, fewer applications will be turned down on grounds of materials and appearance. However, new issues will no doubt arise: new roads, new quarries, new power lines and pipelines are likely sources of difficulty. As yet unthought of conflicts may appear. For example, the wind generation of electricity could well pose a serious threat to nicely exposed Pennine summits—serried ranks of wind generators would not be popular. Reservoirs are dealt with in a later section but they could be major threats to some very lovely and lonely valleys. These are never simple issues, as all sorts of costs fluctuate with time. A valley such as that flooded at Empingham near Oakham may be of much greater value to the nation agriculturally than a Pennine valley, and, as we move towards a national water grid, problems of this kind of evaluation will occur more frequently. Population is notoriously fickle to forecast but a declining population in industrial Lancashire or Yorkshire might mean that pressures will not be as severe as once thought likely. However, increasing motorway access can mean that the demand for second homes may increase (see fig. 36).

Other Parks

Outside the National Park there is still much very lovely country within the Dales as defined in this study. The Forest of Bowland (fig. 5) has been declared an Area of Outstanding Natural Beauty (A.O.N.B.); in 1974 most of this area was placed in Lancashire. As an A.O.N.B. it is eligible for Countryside Commission grant aid but unlike the National Parks it does not have its own planning committee. It has been suggested that Nidderdale, the Washburn valley and the northern Howgills should all be designated as A.O.N.B.[5][6] The Yorkshire and Humberside Economic Planning Council has recommended that the area from the Pennine foothills to the Vale of York should be regarded as green belt and that Country Parks should be sited in this zone.[7] This theme was returned to again in their regional strategy of 1970 when they suggested 'the need now is to see how best to develop the potential of green belts for recreation and visual pleasure and to concentrate the provision of country parks, footpaths, planting . . . etc. in the green belts where they will be nearest to the bulk of the population.'[8]

So far the third tier of park, that of the Country Park, has not appeared within the Dales. The planning authorities are empowered to establish their own parks with an emphasis on leisure and recreation and some such as Penistone Hill in West Yorkshire and Wycoller in Lancashire have been created already. The Countryside Commission can help these parks with grants and has assisted both those mentioned. Such parks, with perhaps more formal provisions for visitors and nearer to densely populated areas, may well be very necessary if some pressure is to be taken off the National Parks.

In a discussion of the recreational and amenity role of the region, the many buildings and parks both public and private that are available must not be forgotten. Many of these spots in fact, provide some of the most intensively visited points: Fountains Abbey and Bolton Priory are two good examples (photo 23, 24). The properties of the National Trust form another very important group of sites of great popularity. The Yorkshire and Humberside regional strategy suggested that Skipton and Ripon, both lying at navigational headwaters, could become much more important recreational inland watering centres.[9] In Skipton's case this is already happening.

What seems to come out of these suggestions is that perhaps the National Park should be to some extent protected against the too violent inroads of large numbers of people from the nearby towns, and that those who want its particular charms sufficiently strongly will have to play the leisure game according to a set of increasingly rigorous rules if the essential qualities of the area of the Park and of other key sites is to survive.

Common Land

There are, surprisingly, large stretches of common lands in the more isolated parts of the Dales. The pre-1974 Reeth Rural District with an area of 73,000 acres had 53,000 acres of common land and Leyburn R.D.C. with an acreage of 71,697 had 10,513 of common.

Access to moorland that is privately owned is an increasing problem: as pressure grows, it is more likely that landowners will insist on only statutory footpaths being used. Hence common land, the function of which within the medieval agricultural system has already been mentioned, has now another very great significance; it is that of providing open space on which the general public has free access. Technically, the land is still common only to the people of the township whose name it probably bears. Ilkley Moor (photo 85) was an exceptional case in which a township bought a great stretch of hillside for the benefit of the town. The photograph shows the heavy use now made of it as revealed by the footpath pattern. Many other greens and commons survived the nineteenth century enclosures and are now registered as commons and they have great social and community value. Most of the highest fells have also remained common to the parishes within which they lie and the rights of the walkers over most of these fells have rarely been queried. All of this is to some extent

85. Ilkley Moor. Gritstone quarries – now disused – and a footpath network on a major area of land to which there is public access. The Grammar School (bottom right) was built after the enclosure of the Cow Pastures. (Cambridge University Collection).

a matter of give and take: hill farmers live by their sheep and the upkeep of walls is a significant element in their costs: if walkers and their dogs respect the sheep and the walls, the hill farmers are less likely to object to the walkers.

Grouse

A clash that has produced a lot of problems has been that between the owners of grouse moors and the public demanding access for walking. The red grouse, indigenous to the moors of the north-west of Britain, became the nineteenth century replacement for the deer. Landowners began to 'farm' their moors in order to produce the best crop of grouse for their shoots and owners of large estates, such as the Duke of Devonshire in Wharfedale have their own moors. Bolton Abbey Gatehouse provides the hunting lodge for the Duke's shooting parties every year from August 12; elsewhere, a moor may be managed for a syndicate of owners and tenants. Access to such moors is strictly controlled during the nesting and shooting seasons. Many of the finest stretches of moor result from the combined techniques of grazing sheep and burning o the old heather that have evolved in order to produce the best feed for young grouse. The great stretches of heather moor, such as that on photo 8 or those in the Forest of Bowland above Slaidburn, form a significant part of the Dales landscape. These heather moors are interrupted only by outcrops of grey, weathered gritstone and occasional lines of shooting butts where the guns are placed to wait the flight of the grouse, set up by keeper-controlled beaters. It is fair to say that sensible compromises over access have now been reached in many such areas.

Water Supply

One of the key attractions of the Dales is that provided by the many fast flowing streams that rise on the wide marshy plateaux and flow off their steep sides in gullies to the floors of the main valleys. The importance of these streams in the location of villages and farms and in the establishment of many water mills in the eighteenth and nineteenth centuries has already been noted. The main rivers too, with their old bridges and riverside walks are also a major feature of the Dales landscape. The water engineer attempting to supply an urban area with a pure water supply must look longingly at an area such as that of the Dales from which comes a plentiful supply of cheap water.

Gregory estimated in 1954 that there was a supply of perhaps 850 million gallons per day available for use in what he termed the North Central Pennines. Of this, he calculated that 55 million gallons a day were being used (excluding privately supplied factories), that is only 6.5 per cent of the available yield: this figure is probably now rather higher. In the Forest of Bowland he calculated 35 million gallons per day out of a possible 260 million was being taken, that is some 13.7 per cent. Those who have looked at the river Dunsop, upstream of Dunsop Bridge, will have seen that this degree of extraction is beginning to have a noticeable effect on the channel of the stream: it is always far drier than the size of the river bed would suggest it should be.[10] The construction of Stocks Reservoir, together with the planting of Gisburn Forest, has had a marked impact on the landscape of the upper valley of the river Hodder.

All estimates of future water use within England show an ever rising demand. A study in 1966 suggested that by 1981 the Yorkshire River Authority would have a deficiency of 90 million gallons a day and this would have risen to one of 335 million gallons a day by 2001.[11] Whilst this authority draws water from the south-central Pennines as well as the north-central, this is clearly going to place a very great increase in demand, much of which will fall on the Dales because the south-central Pennines already have over 20% of their potential tapped. It may be that finally the sheer volume of extra demand will swing the balance of argument about national water provision towards the construction of one or more of the Dee, Morecambe Bay or Solway Barrage schemes. However, it is very likely that as least some new medium term schemes will have to be introduced into the Dales area.

Like so many other British institutions, that of our water supply has undergone many stages of evolution. Local authorities provided local schemes initially and then gradually expanded them if they could. Leeds and Bradford began to look for much more permanent supplies in the latter part of the nineteenth century and they turned their institutional eyes on the Washburn and Upper Nidd valleys respectively. Fig. 37 shows the reservoirs that have been constructed within the Dales. This city need for water has changed the Washburn valley more than any other in the Dales. Leeds Corporation waterworks secured an Act of Parliament in 1867 and Fewston, Swinsty and Lindley Wood reservoirs were constructed. In 1897 the Corporation was empowered to buy much of the Washburn valley and finally in 1966 Thruscross reservoir was completed. A dale has virtually been devoted to the role of supplying water to Leeds. This was still not enough, however, and between 1901 and 1929 Leeds expanded its influence into the Ure valley; a tributary of the Ure, Burn Beck, was used by constructing Leighton reservoir and the river Laver then tapped from works upstream of Ripon.

Bradford cast its eyes on Wharfedale and Nidderdale. An Act of Parliament of 1854 empowered the building of Grimwith and Barden reservoirs in Wharfedale and one of 1870 (1890) gave Bradford its foothold in Nidderdale and led to the construction of three large reservoirs.[12] [13] The quality of the water taken by Bradford was of crucial importance because of the great demands of the woollen textile industry. It is this fact that limited the claims by the textile industry for more reservoirs within the Dales because of the hardness of water derived from the limestones.

The demand for water increases steadily as standards of living rise. The national pressure for an integrated system of supply has resulted in an enlargement of water-providing organisations until we now have a Yorkshire Water Authority and this in turn comes under the Water Resources Board for matters of national policy. Recent reports by the Board have cast their eyes widely over and around the Dales area in listing many possible sites for future reservoirs. All these are interim sites on the assumption that estuary storage will come later as well. Even the enlargement of existing reservoirs such as Grimwith and Gouthwaite in order to allow further extraction will have considerable local impact

86. Scar House Reservoir, Nidderdale, built to supply Bradford.

but the use of Bishopdale, Arkledale or the Hodder valley and its headstreams above Dunsop Bridge would have far greater effects. It is clear that the whole question of water supply is going to create some very important clashes of interest before the end of this century.

Forestry

So far, afforestation has not been the problem in the Yorkshire Dales that it has in the Lake District or in the Kielder Forest of Northumberland. The thin limestone soils, whilst they may locally support ash woodland, are not ideally suited to the growth of conifers: though on the limestones overlooking Morecambe Bay to the west of the Dales, yew woods flourish.

The major areas of afforestation are at the head of Langstrothdale, in the Timble and Fewston areas, around the base of Simon's Fell in Wharfedale on the Devonshire estate and in the Gisburn area. Fine stretches of deciduous woodland survive along the Wharfe between Bolton Abbey and Barden Tower, again on the Devonshire estate, and also on the Swale, upstream from Richmond. The pressure for self-sufficiency in timber is likely to increase and, depending on tax legislation, it would seem likely that more afforestation may be attempted. The Structure Plan points out that the Park can only work by consultation: it has no powers to control forestry within the boundary.

Attitudes to further afforestation in the Dales vary. The Economic Forestry Group has planted over 2,000 acres (922 hectares) in the Oughtershaw area at the head of Langstrothdale.[14] The author is not outraged by this and the economic arguments favouring a reduction of

timber imports are strong. However, J. B. Priestley wrote in strong terms
to *The Times* in 1970 arguing, as many would, that afforestation would
destroy the 'stark magnificence' of the area.[15] The president of the
Country Landowners' Association replied, arguing that 'There are already
upland farms which, if not afforested, will simply be abandoned.'[16]

Quarrying

Quarrying has locally been very important from early times. In the
early nineteenth century it probably reached its peak in the Millstone
Grit areas as population was growing and as water-powered industry was
developing. Some major uses of stone remain: limestone is very valuable
both for agricultural lime and as a raw material for the cement industry.
Fig. 37 shows the locations of working limestone quarries within the
region. One or two quarries such as Ingleton and Horton 'granite' work
the pre-carboniferous Ingletonian and Horton Flags for road metal material
of a very high quality. Limestone is also used as a road metal, although
this is regarded by many as a misuse of it because it means that larger
quantities are being worked within the National Park than would otherwise
be necessary.[17] There is an obvious clash between those wanting no

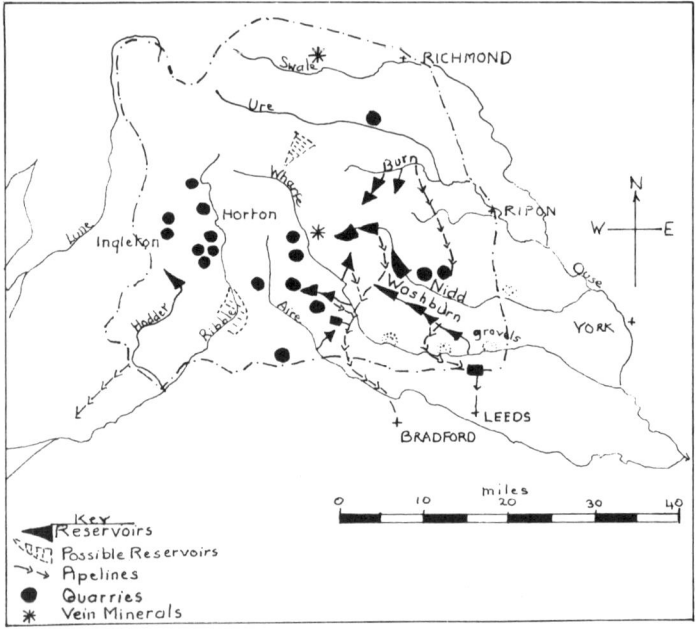

Fig. 37.   Yorkshire Dales water supply and mineral workings.

87. The impact of quarrying in the Dales as seen at Horton-in-Ribblesdale.

spoliation of the 'beautiful and relatively wild' country and those wanting work or needing limestone for industrial processes.[18]

Considerable areas of ancient rock and of limestone had already been secured for future working before the Dales Park was created. It was estimated in 1973/4 that some three million tons of stone are quarried from the Grassington and Ribblesdale areas each year, though this figure has fallen recently. As well as the quarries there is a problem of moving the limestone. This is now done largely by road and the closure of railways that could have moved this ideal rail freight now seems ridiculous. As yet there is no national approach to this problem.[19] If mineral working is shifted from the Park it will almost certainly mean that other areas will come under heavy pressure for new permissions to quarry.

What of the future?

More people and more cars seem certainties until the end of the century. It appears that the population of the United Kingdom is at last stabilising but even given little increase in population, more people in their cars will want to visit areas such as the Dales. Some idea of numbers to be expected comes from the *National Park Policies Review Committee* which cites the example of the Brecon Beacons Mountain Centre. It was expected that 10,000 people would visit it in a year: in 1972, 200,000 people visited it. Improvement of facilities and successful publicity in fact create their own problems of the damage of overuse. Indeed, one senses that the whole of the report is really saying that, if National Parks are to be regarded primarily as areas of high landscape quality, then public amenity may have to come second in the list of priorities of management because environmental quality will suffer if it is given first priority.

It would seem likely that Country Parks on the outer, most accessible edges of the region, Ilkley Moor for example, will be emphasised more in the spending of the County Councils. Certain other areas will, perhaps, be made no more accessible than now—a twisting road with no parking is itself a check to flow of traffic; elsewhere, certain groups such as qualified naturalists may have priority of access. Buses may be made the only way of reaching other parts of the region. However, amongst this increasing pressure of visitors, the local farmers and indigenous population must be encouraged to stay and provide that distinctive way of life that makes the Dales such an interesting and different area for those who want to refresh themselves after a week amongst the noise, dust and concrete of our increasingly similar and depressing cities.

References

J. A. Patmore, *Land and Leisure*, Pelican 1970. A useful introduction to the issues and the literature.

[1] *Report of the National Park Policies Review Committee* (The Sandford Report), Department of the Environment 1974, para. 3.1. Hereafter Sandford Report.

[2] Sandford Report, para. 5.41.

[3] Sandford Report, para. 14.6.

[4] Sandford Report, para. 3.5.

[5] *A Review of Yorkshire and Humberside*, Yorkshire & Humberside Economic Planning Council, H.M.S.O. 1966, Section 10, para. 367 (hereafter Yorks. & Humber).

[6] Geographical Magazine, *Map of Cherished Land*, I.P.C. Magazines, 1973.

[7] Yorks. & Humber., para. 365 and para. 470.

[8] *Yorkshire and Humberside Regional Strategy*, Y. & H. E.P.C., HMSO 1970, para. 281.

[9] Yorks. & Humber., para. 470.

[10] S. Gregory, 'The Contributions of the Uplands to the public water supply of England and Wales', *I.B.G.*, 25, 1958, pp.153–166.

[11] *Morecambe Bay and Solway Barrages*, Water Resources Board, 1966, Fig. i.

[12] B. Jennings, *Nidderdale*, Huddersfield 1967, p.204.

[13] Bradford Corporation Waterworks, *Centenary Handbook 1855–1955*. Copy kindly loaned by E. W. Richardson, Yorkshire Water Authority (Western Division).

[14] *Initial National Park Plan*, Yorkshire Dales National Park Committee, Bainbridge, 1977, p.40, Table 3 (hereafter Park Plan).

[15] Times, 4 March 1970.

[16] Times, 6 March 1970.

[17] *Background*, C.P.R.E. Issue 7/76, quoting Geoffrey Lean, *Yorkshire Post* 20–1, June 1976 (hereafter Lean).

[18] Lean as above.

[19] Park Plan, pp.54–58 and Table 5 and map 9.

INDEX

Places are listed only where more information is given than the name.
Photographs are denoted by ph plus photograph number; Tables by T and Table
number; Figures by f and figure number.

169